ACCOUNTING FOR SMALL BUSINESSES

BUSINESS GUIDEBOOKS

SELF-HELP GUIDES FOR SMALL BUSINESSMEN

ACCOUNTING FOR SMALL BUSINESSES

JACK HELLINGS

SENIOR LECTURER IN ECONOMICS,
MANCHESTER POLYTECHNIC

SERIES FOREWORD BY DAVID TRIPPIER,
UNDER SECRETARY OF STATE AT THE
DEPARTMENT OF INDUSTRY

Sphere Reference

Sphere Reference
30/32 Gray's Inn Road, London WC1X 8JL

First published by
Sphere Books Ltd 1983
Reprinted 1986

Copyright © 1983 Jack Hellings

Typeset by Santype International Ltd, Salisbury, Wilts.
Printed and bound in Great Britain by
Cox & Wyman Ltd, Reading

CONTENTS

SERIES FOREWORD
by David Trippier MP,
Parliamentary Under Secretary of State for Industry

The environment for small businesses has changed greatly for the better in the past four years. An effective Loan Guarantee Scheme and generous tax relief through the Business Expansion Scheme are only two of many in over 100 Government measures to provide incentives and remove obstacles to business enterprise. Our efforts are complemented by a welcome improvement in attitudes in commerce and industry towards the small business operator.

Vital though these changes are, the success of any new expanding business will always depend on the skill, knowledge and tenacity of those running the firm. Practical sources of expertise and advice, as provided by this series of Business Guidebooks, are invaluable aids for the busy entrepreneur. General business management and finance, without doubt, cause the most problems and biggest headaches for the small firm.

Certainly many young businesses have been given a better chance of success by the increasing availability of help with the particular challenges that beset them. I am encouraged by figures which show for the two years, 1981 and 1982, 'births' of new firms well in excess of 'deaths' in spite of the worldwide economic recession.

A flourishing small firms sector in any national economy brings new energy, new enterprise and new initiatives into industry and commerce. These attributes have never been more necessary than in today's tough economic climate and highly competitive world markets. To this end, these Business Guidebooks will be a worth-while investment for every new and expanding business.

Certainly many young businesses have been given a better chance of success by the increasing availability of help with the particular challenges that beset them. I am encouraged by figures which show for the two years, 1981 and 1982, 'births' of new firms well in excess of 'deaths' in spite of the worldwide economic recession.

A flourishing small firms sector in any national economy brings new energy, new enterprise and new initiatives into industry and commerce. These attributes have never been more necessary than in today's tough economic climate and highly competitive world markets. To this end, these Business Guidebooks will be a worthwhile investment for every new and expanding business.

INTRODUCTION

This book is not written for students of accounting but for practising managers. In particular it is addressed to those who are the sole executive within their firm. Filling the roles of buyer, production controller, sales manager and chief administrator leaves little time for anything except the essentials. This is our purpose—to present the essentials of accounting for small businesses.

The first seven chapters cover all financial accounting procedures down to Final Accounts. There follows a chapter on commercial systems and two chapters on the use of accounting data for planning purposes. This total of ten chapters covers all that is needed for those who sell, as opposed to manufacture, goods.

Next there are nine chapters on cost accounting. These are designed to set out a complete costing system for those who manufacture goods or sell services. If the financial accounting chapters are omitted Chapter 9 will need to be read, preferably between Chapters 15 and 16.

After costing the problem of pricing is considered. An efficient pricing system depends upon an efficient costing system. Some of the mysteries are, it is hoped, removed from planning and control before we conclude with two chapters on measuring performance.

Finally thanks are due to all colleagues and students, past and present, for their help in writing this book, and to Jean Hellings for all her work on the manuscript.

Jack Hellings

1. SALES AND ACCOUNTS

Business consists of a series of transactions:

Buying   **Selling**   **Paying bills**   **Cashing cheques**

At first sight this list may seem to contain four changes but in fact there are eight changes.

Suppose you buy goods for cash. Two changes occur. You now have less money and more goods.

Selling for cash means less goods, more cash.

If you have received a bill the organisation sending it is one of your creditors. When you pay you have less creditors and less cash.

When you cash a cheque you are drawing out from your bank account. Now you have more cash, less in the bank.

Although only four examples are given it is always true that there are two sides to every transaction. If we are to keep proper books we must record both aspects, in fact this is the origin of the name **Double Entry Book-keeping**.

As you will have seen some transactions mean more of something and less of another. But you should not run away with the idea that this is always so. Paying a bill has been shown to be a transaction in which both sides are reduced. We shall not set out a general rule for you to apply to each transaction. Instead we shall set out a specific rule to deal with each type of transaction likely to be met in running a small business.

The actual documents forming the accounts may take a number of forms. Originally bound books were used. Each page was numbered, and the page for a particular account was found by reference to an index. As you can imagine, even for the smallest firm, this method is hardly practical.

The first alternative is the **loose-leaf system**. Each account uses a single page and all pages are filed in a binder. The advantage over the bound book is that new pages can be inserted in alphabetical, or other predetermined, order. The binder may be lockable so that only senior people are able to insert or remove sheets.

The second alternative is to keep accounts on **cards**. These are about twelve inches square and are kept in some form of filing tray. As with loose-leaf methods they are arranged in appropriate order. When an entry has to be made the card is withdrawn; afterwards it is returned to its place. This system offers the same advantages as the loose-leaf method, but has the disadvantage that there is less control over used and unused sheets. This method is usually associated with the use of accounting machines, but also forms the basis of some manual systems. A more detailed examination of these is given in Chapter 8.

The third alternative involves all the methods used in **computerised accounts**. As we assume that these systems are for the larger firms we shall not discuss them here.

From our point of view it does not matter at the outset whether we imagine ourselves to be using a card or loose-leaf system. Both will be ruled in the manner of Exhibit 1.1. As this form will be used in all our book-keeping it is as well to consider it very carefully.

There are twelve columns, divided into two sets of six by a double line. The first set has been headed up to show its use. The date takes up the first two columns. The year is not shown against each entry, only the month and day. It is essential that all book-keeping entries are dated, if for no other reason than to distinguish between several items of the same amount. Such duplications occur more often than you might think.

The wide column is used for cross-reference between accounts. As we have already discovered the need to record both sides of a transaction it follows that any ledger entry records only one aspect. In the cross-reference column we write the name of the account in which the second entry is made. The usefulness of this will be appreciated as we proceed.

This leaves us with columns for pounds and pence to complete each entry. The same ruling is then repeated and the obvious way to distinguish them is to call them **Left-hand Side** and **Right-hand Side**. This will be abbreviated to **LHS** and **RHS** from now on.

The heading is in the middle and refers to both sides and is the name of the **account**. Shortly we shall be using Sales Account and VAT Account. As every page is an account there is little point in writing Account after everything. So we will merely head accounts 'Sales', 'VAT', and so on in all our examples.

We are now ready to record actual transactions. Because we are interested in the method we shall make simplifications in other directions. VAT varies from time to time. Who knows what it will be at the time you are reading this book? So let us use a rate of 10% because this rate simplifies our calculations. All calculations of VAT that follow will be to the nearest penny, at the 10% rate.

Our first transaction is the sale of goods. We assume that goods are sold to a long-standing customer, the terms of the sale being '30 days net'. This means that in thirty days time we shall receive payment or, put the other way round, the customer will be in our debt for thirty days. If a firm is in our debt it is a **debtor**. As we shall receive cash from them in due course our debtors are as much an asset as is our cash.

2

When goods are despatched an invoice will be sent with them, separately the same day, or at worst within one day of despatch. There will be considerable detail on the invoice but we are only interested in

EXHIBIT 1·1

				HEADING					
DATE	CROSS·REFERENCE	FOLIO	£	P					
19×1									
JAN 1									

EXHIBIT 1·2

19×1			E. SMITH LTD.						
MAR 10	SALES & V.A.T	33	–						
			SALES						
				19×1					
				MAR 10	E. SMITH LTD.		30	–	
			V.A.T.						
				19×1					
				MAR 10	E. SMITH LTD.		3	–	

3

certain facts. These are the details we would take for book-keeping purposes.

Customer's Name		E Smith Ltd
Date		10th March 19x1
Amounts	Goods	£30·00
	VAT	£3·00
	TOTAL	£33·00

The book-keeping entries are shown in Exhibit 1.2. In this example we must open three accounts, in the real world there would probably be accounts already opened.

A separate account will be needed for every customer. It should be headed with the full, exact name of the customer. 'Smith' will not do. Even if now you have only one customer called Smith you may get others, and then inaccurate naming of accounts will cause endless trouble. The total amount of the invoice will be entered on LHS of the customer's account.

The Sales Account entry is on RHS for goods only. The VAT amount is entered on the RHS of the VAT account. Every sale will require the same set of entries.

LHS	Customer's account	Total amount
RHS	Sales accounts	Goods amount
RHS	VAT account	VAT amount

Note that **entries on LHS = RHS entries**. In this case $33 = 30 + 3$. This will always be true, and so we shall get at least a rough check on the accuracy of our work.

As we go on undertaking transactions, in this case making sales, so the totals on these accounts will tell us something important about the business as a whole.

Without giving full details let us assume that we have sent different customers twenty invoices for goods. These were for goods selling for £800, on which there is VAT of £80 due.

After these have been recorded in the same way as for E Smith Ltd our accounts would show:

Accounts for twenty customers totalling	£880	LHS
Sales account entries totalling	£800	RHS
VAT account entries totalling	£80	RHS

As before LHS = RHS ($880 = 800 + 80$)

This is expressing it in accounting terms; let us put it in everyday business terms.

Our accounts show that we have sold goods for £800, and we owe

4

VAT of £80 on these sales. Twenty customers owe us a total of £880. (To revert to accounting terms these are our debtors.)

This relatively simple method of recording credit sales gives the owner a lot of useful information, indeed if the business is to run at maximum profitability it is essential information.

The book-keeping needed when customers pay is dealt with later.

Book-keeping Summary

When goods are invoiced to customers:

Side	Account	Amount
LHS	Customer	Invoice total
RHS	Sales	Goods only
RHS	VAT	VAT only

Totals on accounts indicate:

Side	Account	Meaning
LHS	Customer	Owing to you—Debtor
RHS	Sales	Value of goods sold
RHS	VAT	VAT owed

2. SUPPLIERS AND ACCOUNTS

In this chapter we shall cover the actions to take when goods are purchased, and how to deal with cash transactions.

The term **Purchases** has a restricted meaning as far as book-keeping is concerned which is best explained by examples.

    (i) A retailer buys stock to re-sell.
    (ii) A manufacturer buys raw material to process and sell in the form of finished goods.
    (iii) A retailer buys a year's supply of printed stationery.
    (iv) A manufacturer buys a new machine.

The term purchases is restricted to (i) and (ii). The question to be asked is '. . . is object obtained for resale?'. If the answer is yes then, from the book-keeping point of view, it comes under the heading of Purchases. If the answer is no it is not Purchases. Example (iii) is the buying of something which will be used up in the course of business, but not sold to customers. Example (iv) is the buying of something to be kept and used in the business. As with (iii) the machine will not be sold to customers.

So (i) and (ii) are Purchases; (iii) and (iv) are, respectively, **Expenses** and **Assets**. Their treatment will be dealt with later.

Let us assume now that on April 12th 19x1, Jones Manufacturing Ltd have delivered goods and sent us an invoice for £200 plus VAT of £20, making £220 in all. What steps should we take? Unlike Sales there are things to be done before we can do the book-keeping. These can be summarised as follows:

1. Check Order. Have these goods been ordered? Is the quantity, and the price correct? Are the terms (discount etc.) correct?

2. Check Delivery. Do the goods delivered correspond with the invoice and order? Have they in fact arrived?

3. Check Calculations. Have the individual items been multiplied out, and then added up, correctly? Is the VAT calculation correct?

Assuming we are satisfied that we should accept the invoice we now proceed with the book-keeping entries. For our example they will be as in Exhibit 2.1. The entries may be summarised as we did for sales:

EXHIBIT 2.1

JONES MANUFACTURING LTD

					19x1				
					APR	12	PURCHASES & V.A.T	220	–

PURCHASES

19x1									
APR	12	JONES MFG. LTD.	200	–					

V.A.T.

19x1									
APR	12	JONES MFG. LTD.	20	–					

EXHIBIT 2.2.

V.A.T.

19x1					19x1				
APR	12	JONES MFG. LTD.	20	–	MAR	10	E. SMITH LTD.	3	–

LHS   Purchases account   Goods amount
LHS   VAT account   VAT amount
RHS   Supplier's account   Total amount

As before LHS = RHS (200 + 20 = 220).

In Exhibit 2.1, we show an account for VAT. In the real world only one VAT account is kept. If the transactions with E Smith Ltd and Jones Manufacturing Ltd were the only ones undertaken the account for VAT would be as rewritten, Exhibit 2.2.

We can suppose as before that there are a number of accounts for suppliers. On going through our ledger we find:

Accounts for twelve suppliers totalling	£660	RHS
Purchases account entries totalling	£600	LHS
VAT account entries totalling	£60	LHS

These entries tell us that we owe £660 to people who have sold us goods for re-sale. Of this £600 is for the actual goods and £60 represents VAT we will deduct from our own VAT payment.

When we owe money we have **creditors**. It is important that we know the total of our creditors, and when we must pay, otherwise we can find ourselves in serious trouble. As we proceed we shall consider ways of avoiding **cash flow problems** of this nature.

Now we shall consider how to deal with cash transactions, and the easiest point to begin is with cash sales. As there is considerable similarity with sales on credit it is to be expected that the entries will be similar.

In fact the entries in Sales and VAT accounts are similar, and all three entries are shown in Exhibit 2.3. The sales are for £20 plus VAT of £2, on 20th May 19x1.

The summarised entries are:

LHS	Cash account	Total amount
RHS	Sales account	Goods amount
RHS	VAT account	VAT amount

The Sales entries will be on the one account which accommodates all entries, and the same is true of VAT.

In the last chapter, and in the beginning of this, we considered credit transactions. Both must eventually lead to cash changing hands.

On the 10th April 19x1 we receive a cheque for £33 from E Smith Ltd. A little thought will bring us to the conclusion that we wish to cancel the debt on this firm's account. We can do this by a RHS entry of £33. We record the receipt of cash in the same way as for a cash sale by a LHS entry of £33 in the cash account.

So our general rule becomes:

LHS	Cash account	Amount received
RHS	Customer's account	Amount received

EXHIBIT 2.3.

19x1						CASH							
MAY	20	SALES & V.A.T.		22	–								

						SALES							
							19x1						
							MAY	20	CASH			20	–

						VAT							
							19x1						
							MAY	20	CASH			2	–

EXHIBIT 2.4

19x1						E. SMITH LTD.	19x1						
MAR	10	SALES & VAT		33	–	APR	10	CASH			33	–

19x1						CASH							
APR	10	E. SMITH LTD.		33	–							

EXHIBIT 2.5

19x1						JONES MANUFACTURING LTD.	19x1						
MAY	12	CASH		220	–	APR	12	PURCHASES & V.A.T.	220	–

						CASH							
							19x1				
							MAY	12	JONES MFG. LTD	220	–

EXHIBIT 2.6

19x1						BANK	19x1						
JUNE	1	BALANCE		1,000		JUNE	3	CASH			80	–

19x1						CASH							
JUNE	1	BALANCE		97	20						
	3	BANK		80	–						

The entries are shown in Exhibit 2.4. The customer's account should be compared with that of Exhibit 1.2.

Book-keeping is quite a logical procedure. If we enter cash received on the LHS it is logical to enter cash paid on the RHS. If we show a creditor as an RHS entry when we pay him we will make a LHS entry. And this reasoning tells us the book-keeping entries to make on 12th April 19x1 when we pay Jones Manufacturing Ltd what we owe on 12th May.

LHS	Supplier's account	Amount paid
RHS	Cash account	Amount paid

The original entry, Exhibit 2.1, is shown again, but after payment, in Exhibit 2.5.

It is worth spending a little time comparing the accounts of E Smith Ltd and Jones Manufacturing Ltd. In any small firm a very high proportion of book-keeping entries will relate to sales and purchases so being quite clear about these entries is important.

This chapter will close with one more transaction, cashing a cheque. All firms will have a bank current account, and so they will need a separate Cash account and Bank account in their books. Normally payments to and from suppliers and customers will be by cheque. If this had been the case in our two examples, Exhibits 2.4 and 2.5, the entry in a Cash account would appear instead in a Bank account.

Cashing a cheque may not appear to be a transaction in the sense this has been defined so far. However, the bank is third party just as, say E Smith Ltd is a third party. After cashing a cheque we shall have less in the bank and more in our till or cash box. The entries are quite straightforward and it is a help to remember the definition of a debtor. This is someone who owes you money. Your bank is in the same position as a debtor, albeit a rather special debtor.

When E Smith Ltd made a payment our entries were:

Exhibit 2.4.   LHS   Cash account : RHS   Smith's account

Cashing a cheque is the same as the bank making a payment to you so we get:

LHS	Cash account	Amount of cash
RHS	Bank account	Amount of cash

This transaction appears in Exhibit 2.6, which assumes a bank balance of £1,000, a cash balance of £97·20 and a cheque cashed on 3rd June for £80.

It is suggested that you should decide for yourselves the entries to record paying in cash to the bank, an operation carried out by most retailers at frequent intervals. The answer can be checked against the Summary.

Book-keeping Summary

When goods are invoiced by suppliers:

Side	Account	Amount
LHS	Purchases	Goods only
LHS	VAT	VAT only
RHS	Supplier	Invoice total

Totals on accounts indicate:

Side	Account	Meaning
LHS	Purchases	Value of goods purchased
LHS	VAT	VAT deductable
RHS	Supplier	Owing from you = Creditor

Payments from customers:

Side	Account	Amount
LHS	Cash or Bank	Payment received
RHS	Customer	Payment received

Payment to suppliers:

Side	Account	Amount
LHS	Supplier	Payment total
RHS	Cash or Bank	Payment total

Bank transactions:

Cashing cheque	LHS Cash account	RHS Bank account
Paying in cash	LHS Bank account	RHS Cash account

Bank's relationship to you:

Debtor	When you have cash in the bank
Creditor	When you have an overdraft

Suppliers invoices:
No invoice should be entered in the accounts until it has been checked.
There are really three questions:

1. Do goods agree with your order?
2. Have the goods invoiced actually been delivered?
3. Has the invoice been correctly calculated?

3. TRADE AND CASH DISCOUNTS

In this chapter we shall be dealing with the treatment of **discounts**. These may be **Trade Discounts** or **Cash Discounts**, and they will be dealt with in that order.

Some firms sell their products to wholesalers, retailers and to the general public. Obviously there is a different price to each section of their market; retailers would not be happy if a manufacturer charged them the same price charged to the general public.

This state of affairs could give rise to three different price lists: Wholesale List, Retail List, Direct Sales List. The need for anything as costly as this is overcome by using a single list, of the highest prices, and deducting discount according to the status of the purchaser. It is this deduction which is known as Trade Discount. It is deducted from the total of the invoice. This means that it is never included in the accounts.

Although Trade Discount, if allowable, is always deducted the same is not true of Cash Discount. This can be described briefly as an allowance for prompt payment. A purchaser is not always required to pay at once. The account may be payable in, say, one month. Provided it is paid within that time the customer may deduct a stated percentage. It is this that is the Cash Discount.

Generally speaking people refer to **Terms**. '$2\frac{1}{2}\%$ one month' are the terms operated by many suppliers. Provided the account is settled within one month $2\frac{1}{2}\%$ is deducted from the invoice value of the goods. Not, be it noted, from the VAT, treatment of which will be explained shortly.

Firms are not always free to fix their own Terms. Readers already in business will know that there are often Trade Terms generally adhered to within a particular area, and cash discounts are often fixed within the industry.

We shall now consider four alternatives, and in so doing the treatment of VAT will be shown.

Goods valued at £100 are invoiced. Totals will be shown:

   (i) No Trade or Cash Discount
  (ii) 20% Trade Discount, no Cash Discount
 (iii) 5% Cash Discount, no Trade Discount
 (iv) 5% Cash Discount, 20% Trade Discount

(i)

	£
Goods	100
VAT	10
	£110

(ii)

	£
Goods	100
less 20% Trade Discount	20
	80
VAT	8
	£88

Note that in this case VAT is calculated net of Trade Discount, i.e. Trade Discount is deducted before VAT is calculated.

(iii)

	£
Goods	100·00
VAT	9·50
	£109·50

Where Cash Discount is allowable VAT is calculated on the net Cash Discount figure.

i.e.

	£
Goods	100·00
less 5% Cash Discount	5·00
	£95·00
VAT at 10%	£9·50

Even if Cash Discount is not deducted VAT is still calculated in this way.

(iv)

	£
Goods	100·00
less 20% Trade Discount	20·00
	80·00
plus VAT	7·60
	£87.60

	£
The VAT calculation is	
Goods less Trade Discount	80·00
less 5% Cash Discount	4·00
	£76·00
VAT at 10%	£7·60

Where adjustments have been made for discounts the calculation of VAT is relatively simple. But remember when paying accounts Cash Discount must only be deducted from the goods figure not from the invoice total.

Book-keeping Summary

The book-keeping entries for sales and purchases are as stated in Chapters 1 and 2. The following table is to assist in the calculation of sales invoice totals.

Discount		Goods	VAT
Trade	Cash		
No	No	Selling Price	% of Selling Price
Yes	No	Selling Price less Trade Discount	% of Selling Price less Trade Discount
No	Yes	Selling Price	% of Selling Price less Cash Discount
Yes	Yes	Selling Price less Trade Discount	% of Selling Price less Trade Discount and Cash Discount

4. OTHER ACCOUNTS

So far we have dealt with the book-keeping for buying and selling goods. But even the smallest business could not be carried on without entering into other types of transaction.

The business would need premises and this would involve paying out cash for rent. Transactions of this type are referred to as **Expenses**. Postage, stationery, electricity, running costs of vehicles are all examples of expenses. Of course a firm has to cover all of its expenses out of its sales revenue if it is to make a profit. This alone is sufficient reason for us to want a clear and full record of the firm's expenses.

The other principal type of transaction is the **purchase of assets**. A retailer will need a counter, shelving and display cabinets. A cash register and a van for deliveries are not uncommon. A manufacturer will need storage facilities for raw materials and finished goods, machinery, and perhaps a fork-lift truck. Both retailers and manufacturers will need typewriters, filing cabinets and probably adding machines and/or calculators. There is a lot of money tied up in **Fixed Assets**, as they are called, and a firm ought to know how that amount is made up.

For us it will be easier to start with the purchase of assets. As explained in Chapter 2, we do not treat the buying of assets as part of Purchases. This latter term is only used in the case of goods for re-sale. We shall have to open some new accounts when assets are first acquired. Let us suppose that our firm is buying a delivery van. It will be handing over a cheque for £6,500 when the vehicle is delivered on 12th July 19x1.

An account must be opened for Delivery Vans, and the entries will be:

LHS	Delivery Vans account	Amount paid
RHS	Bank account	Amount paid

The Delivery Vans account, and an extract from the Bank account are shown in Exhibit 4.1.

As many separate accounts will be opened as are necessary. Each account will be for a distinct category of assets. If our firm purchased a motor car it may be considered necessary to open a Motor Cars account. It would then have a separate record of the amount spent on vans and cars. Probably it would not need so much detail, in which case it would use a single Motor Vehicles account and enter the cost of both vehicles on LHS of this account.

The firm will have a series of accounts, one for each category of asset. The accounts will show, on LHS, the cost to the firm of assets

EXHIBIT 4.1

19x1			DELIVERY VANS.							
JULY	12	BANK	6,500	–						
			BANK		(EXTRACT)					
					19x1					
					JULY	12	DELIVERY VANS	6,500	–	

EXHIBIT 4.2

19x1			BANK							
AUG	1	CAPITAL ACCOUNT	10,000							
			CAPITAL	ACCOUNT						
					19x1					
					AUG	1	BANK	10,000	–	

of each category. For the time being these balances will simply stay there unaltered as a record of expenditure. Their treatment when calculating profit and preparing balance sheets will be considered later.

When thinking of expenses it is easy enough to build up a long list. Wages and Rates are two examples, one occuring every week and the

20

other once, or perhaps twice, a year. In the first case the payment will be in cash.

| LHS | Wages account | Amount paid |
| RHS | Cash account | Amount paid |

The second example will probably be paid by cheque.

| LHS | Rates account | Amount paid |
| RHS | Bank account | Amount paid |

The cash holding, or bank balance, will be reduced by the amounts paid and there will be a number of accounts with amounts on the LHS which together will represent all the firm's payments for expenses. How these are dealt with at the end of the year will be shown subsequently.

You will see that so far we have made a variety of entries on LHS. The Book-keeping Summary lists these in full and from this it will be possible to say what each entry or total represents. It must be emphasised that every figure in the books has a real meaning. Thus a LHS entry on a customer's account tells you that he owes this amount. When payment is made the RHS entry on the customer's account will cancel out the LHS entry. The account then shows that the customer is no longer one of our debtors.

A LHS entry on an account whose name indicates an asset shows how much the firm has spent on that type of asset. Shop premises, warehouse fittings, machinery, delivery vans, and office equipment are all examples of assets.

Other LHS entries will bear the names of running costs. Rent, wages, insurance, stationery, light and power, and telephone charges will serve as examples of this category.

There should be no difficulty in distinguishing between Assets and Expenses. The cost of buying a delivery van is clearly the cost of acquiring an asset. The cost of running that asset, equally clearly, is an expense of conducting the business.

As we are increasing the number of types of account it is convenient to introduce the account of the owner. At first sight it may appear that we have the entries on the wrong side, but you must remember that our accounting is for the firm not the owner.

Suppose a business is being started from scratch. There are no premises, no machinery, no stock. The owner has £10,000 which he proposes investing in the firm. He opens a bank account for the firm. We need to record both sides of this transaction, which can be summarised as:

1. The firm has an asset of £10,000 in the bank.
2. The firm owes its proprietor £10,000.

Notice that both aspects of this transaction are expressed from the firm's point of view, not that of the owner. These are the book-keeping entries:

LHS	Bank account	Amount paid in
RHS	Proprietor's account	Amount paid in

They are set out in Exhibit 4.2. The proprietor's account is called the **Capital Account**. This is one of the few cases where the word account is actually used. This is because Capital is used in a variety of different ways and saying Capital Account removes any doubt as to what is meant.

When a proprietor pays in any additional funds the entry will be the same. When funds are drawn out the entries will be reversed.

LHS	Capital account	Amount withdrawn
RHS	Bank account	Amount withdrawn

We have now covered all of the recording side of book-keeping. After looking at a few time saving methods we will consider how to calculate profit.

Book-keeping Summary

Purchase of Assets:

Side	Account	Amount
LHS	Asset	Sum paid
RHS	Cash or Bank	Sum paid
Separate accounts for each class of asset		

Payment of Expenses:

Side	Account	Amount
LHS	Expense	Sum paid
RHS	Cash or Bank	Sum paid
Separate accounts for each class of expense		

Proprietor's funds:

(i) Paid in to firm:

Side	Account	Amount
LHS RHS	Bank Capital	Invested Invested

(ii) Withdrawn from firm:

Side	Account	Amount
LHS RHS	Capital Bank	Dis-invested Dis-invested

5. SAVING WORK AND TIME

Let us begin by considering the entries required when goods are invoiced to customers:

LHS	Customer's account	Total amount
RHS	Sales account	Goods amount
RHS	VAT account	VAT amount

Each invoice for goods delivered requires three entries. Normally a month contains twenty two working days. Even if a firm despatches only one consignment each day it will need 22 × 3 = 66 book-keeping entries, unless we adopt a work-saving procedure. Below are listed all the details required for five invoices, which would represent sales for one week in our small firm example. No cash discount is allowed.

Date 19x1	Customer	Goods	VAT	Total
Sep 1	B J Manufacturing Ltd	105·00	10·50	115·50
2	Colin Clarke & Co	65·20	6·52	71·72
3	Greyling (Wholesale) Ltd	948·72	94·87	1,043·59
4	Thomsen Sub-Machine Gun Co	19·85	1·99	21·84
5	Stockton Engineering Co Ltd	320·00	32·00	352·00
		£1,458·77	£145·88	£1,604·65

We can now set about saving time. We enter the "Total" amounts on the LHS of each customer's account. But we do not enter the individual items for "Goods" and "VAT" on the RHS of these accounts. Instead we enter only the totals of these two columns. The actual entries are given below and you should check that both ways result in the same amount being entered in the accounts and that the total LHS still equals the total RHS.

		£	£
LHS	B J Manufacturing Ltd	115·50	
	Colin Clarke & Co	71·72	
	Greyling (Wholesale) Ltd	1,043·59	
	Thomsen Sub-Machine Gun Co	21·84	
	Stockton Engineering Co Ltd	352·00	
RHS	Sales		1,458·77
	VAT		145·88
	Totals	£1,604·65	£1,604·65

In this way the need for fifteen entries has been reduced to a requirement for seven.

We can draw up a table, for various numbers of invoices per month, to show the savings.

Invoices per month	At 3 entries each	Using totals
22	66	24
50	150	52
75	225	77
100	300	102

As a rough guide this method saves two entries out of three, i.e. the work load is reduced by $66\frac{2}{3}\%$. Well worth it—even for the smallest firm.

There is no reason why this method should not be used by retail concerns. The total of cash sales will be known each day and the appropriate entry made on LHS of the Cash or Bank accounts. But nothing is entered on RHS of the Sales or VAT accounts until the end of the month, when the entry on the month's total can be made.

The book in which these entries are made is called the **Sales Journal**. Entering of invoices in this journal should be the first step in accounting for sales. At this stage we can also explain the use of the Folio column. (See Exhibit 1.1.) The pages of the sales journal will be numbered, with an abbreviation to indicate the journal. The invoice to E Smith Ltd (Exhibit 1.2) will have been entered in the Sales Journal, say on the first page, SJ1. It is this reference that is entered in the Folio column. Whenever a query arises on any account, details can be found by referring to the book of original entry, in this case the sales journal. A spare column on the right of our example could be used to enter the reference number of the customer's account, and such a numbering system is well worth undertaking.

This system of sales journals can be extended to purchases. But here an even more useful task can be undertaken. As already indicated the firm must buy goods for resale or processing. This results in a LHS entry on the Purchases account. It will also purchase assets and then the LHS entry will be in the appropriate Asset account. It will also receive accounts for garages, printers, and various service companies. Here the LHS entry will be in the appropriate Expense account. Many expenses are paid in cash it is true but some, at least, will need account entries. From this you may get an inkling of the way the Purchases Journal can be arranged. Here are three invoices:

	19x1		
Sep	10	Engineering Supplies Ltd	£250·00 (+ VAT £25·00)
	12	The Helpful Garage Co	£187·00 (+ VAT £18·70)
	14	B J Robinson	£90·00 (+ VAT £8·55)

These invoices are for a new machine, bill for a month's petrol and service, and raw materials for the factory respectively. The last is subject to 5% Cash Discount. They represent an asset, an expense, and a purchase for eventual resale. Exhibit 5.1 shows a specimen ruling for a purchases journal. Follow the entries one by one.

First the invoice total, VAT, and goods amounts are entered. As the invoice is for an asset the goods amount is extended in the Assets column.

Secondly the invoice total, VAT, and goods amounts are entered. The goods amount is extended to the Expenses column.

Thirdly the same procedure is adopted but here the goods amount is entered under Purchases.

Because of its nature the Purchases Journal is sometimes called the **Purchases Analysis Book**.

Normally the Journal would be added and ruled off at the end of the month. Here it has been ruled off for demonstration purposes.

First notice the relationship between the column totals.

$$\begin{aligned}
\text{Invoice} &= \text{VAT} + \text{Goods} \\
(£579·25) &= (£52·25 + £527) \\
\text{Goods} &= \text{Purchases} + \text{Expenses} + \text{Assets} \\
(£527) &= (£90 + £187 + £250)
\end{aligned}$$

You should always total up and cross-check the columns. Mistakes in writing up the sales journal should then show up.

The book-keeping entries from the Purchase Journal are as follows:

LHS	VAT	Total VAT account
	Purchases	Total Purchases account
	Expenses	Individual accounts
	Assets	Individual accounts
RHS	Invoice amount	Individual suppliers accounts

It would be a useful exercise if you entered these items on accounts. You would find that:

LHS entries = RHS entries = £579·25

Before moving on it is worth making three further points.

First the Purchase Journal may have as many columns as you wish. Suppose the firm packs goods in cardboard boxes and brown paper.

EXHIBIT S.1.			PURCHASES				JOURNAL								
DATE		SUPPLIER	INVOICE		V.A.T.		GOODS		PURCHASES		EX.PS		ASSETS	
1981														
5EP	10	ENG. SUPS. LTD	275	–	25	–	250	–					250	–
	12	HELPFUL GARAGE	205	70	18	70	187	–			187	–		
	14	B.J. ROBINSON	98	55	8	55	90	–	90	–				
			£579	25	£52	25	£527	–	£ 90	–	£187	–	£250	–
EXHIBIT S.2														
SEP.	14	B.J. ROBINSON	98	55	8	55	90	–	81	–	9	–		

It may get weekly deliveries of both items from different suppliers. This means there will be eight to ten entries each month. In this case a Packing Materials column could be used. Then the total of this column will be entered on the LHS of the expense account at the end of the month saving seven to nine entries.

Secondly the Sales Journal may be made analytical. The firm may wish to analyse sales by department, by sales areas or by particular products. Additional columns may be added, and this is quite a useful way of doing things. However, remember that these extra columns are solely for analysis. No figures from these columns are entered in the accounts.

Finally invoices may be split between columns. Suppose B J Robinson was providing 10 cans of paint at £9 + VAT each. One of these the firm is going to use for painting the factory. That is an expense, usually called Repairs and Maintenance. The remainder of the cans will be used in manufacturing and so are Purchases for book-keeping purposes. This is shown in Exhibit 5.2. Invoices can be split between as many columns as necessary, although it is unlikely that more than two columns will be involved.

We close this chapter with two more journals dealing with a matter so far not discussed.

No matter how careful we are there will always be some of our deliveries rejected. Some or all of a consignment may be damaged or sub-standard. Or we may have made a mistake and delivered more than was ordered or even delivered something not ordered at all. Of course the same will be true for our suppliers. The first are called Sales Returns and the second Purchases Returns.

When goods were sold the entries were:

> LHS   Customer's account   RHS   Sales account

Logically we would expect to reverse the entries when the goods are returned, but there is a slight alteration.

> LHS   Sales Returns   RHS   Customer's account

The effect of the entries for the customer should be understandable by now. The total owed shows up on the LHS so a RHS entry reduces the amount shown as owed. Which is, of course, what a return of goods does.

At the end of the year we do this little sum:

Goods sold	RHS = Sales
less Goods returned	LHS = Sales Returns
	RHS − LHS = Sales less returns

This way the Sales account, and Sales Returns account, will be kept separately throughout the year.

The reader is invited to supply the entries for Purchases Returns, which can then be checked against the Book-keeping Summary.

Book-keeping Summary

The book-keeping entries for Sales and customers and for Purchases and suppliers remain as already detailed. The use of journals represent an addition to, not an alteration of, the system described so far.

Entering accounts from Sales Journal:

Side	Account	Amount
LHS	Individual Customer	Invoice
RHS	Sales	Journal total
RHS	VAT	Journal total

Entering accounts from Sales Returns Journal:

Side	Account	Amount
LHS	Sales Returns	Journal total
LHS	VAT	Journal total
RHS	Individual Customer	Value of returns, Goods + VAT

Entering accounts from Purchases Journal:

Side	Account	Amount
*LHS	Purchases	Journal total
LHS	VAT	Journal total
RHS	Individual Supplier	Invoice

* If Analysis Columns are kept the first entry becomes:

LHS	Purchases	Journal total of purchases
LHS	Individual Expense	Items in Expense column
LHS	Individual Asset	Items in Assets column

Entering accounts from Purchases Returns Journal:

Side	Account	Amount
LHS	Individual Supplier	Value of Goods + VAT
RHS	Purchases Returns	Journal total
RHS	VAT	Journal total

6. CLOSING THE BOOKS

Having completed the basic book-keeping we now turn our attention, in this and the next chapter, to calculating profit for the year. In order to do this we must introduce two book-keeping terms not used so far.

The ledger is divided into two sides which we have called LHS and RHS. In the following example, when selling goods, we have three entries:

LHS, enter total amount in customer's account
RHS, enter goods amount in Sales account
RHS, enter VAT in VAT account

Accountants call **LHS the DEBIT side**
and call **RHS the CREDIT side**.

It is easy enough to re-write the instruction just given:

DEBIT   total amount to customer's account
CREDIT goods amount to Sales account
CREDIT VAT amount to VAT account

Entries on LHS, the Debit side, are referred to as **debiting** the account.

Entries on RHS, the Credit side, are referred to as **crediting** the account.

So the mysterious business of Debiting/Crediting means simply entering on LHS/RHS. The usual abbreviations are **DR** and **CR**. To emphasise this fact we shall write in future LHS(DR) and RHS(CR). It may help you to put Debit and Credit at the top of the ledger pages until you are used to the idea.

Before we can calculate profit there is one job we cannot avoid.

Exhibit 6.1 shows one account going through a number of separate stages. Begin with 6.1a.

The fact that (i) it is in the name of a firm (ii) it is a LHS(DR) entry and (iii) it is cross-referenced to Sales and VAT accounts, tells you that this is the account of a customer who owes you £300.

Now the customer returns goods and a RHS(CR) entry is made. More briefly the account has been credited. After this the customer owes only £300 less £20 equals £280. It is easy enough to work out how much a customer owes you by taking the RHS(CR) figures from the LHS(DR) figures. That is to say it is easy enough if there are only two, or at

most three or four, entries involved. If there are more, and if they are
odd figures of pounds and pence, it is much more difficult. When we
come to calculate profit we will use the accounts we have been writing-up
over the year. But we do not want to have to stop every so often to
add up and take away, so we must work through all the accounts to

EXHIBIT

6·1·a

DR.					H. GROVE & CO.					CR
JAN	1	SALES & V.A.T.	300	–						

6·1·b.

JAN	1	SALES & VAT.	300	–	JAN	15	RETURNS		20	–

6·1·c.

JAN	1	SALES & V.A.T.	300	–	JAN	15	RETURNS		20	–
						31	BALANCE C/D		280	–
			£300	–					£300	–

6·1·d

JAN	1	SALES & V.A.T.	300	–	JAN	15	RETURNS		20	–
						31	BALANCE C/D		280	–
			£300	–					£300	–
JAN	31	BALANCE B/D.	280	–						

34

begin with so that every one finishes with only a single figure. The first step is shown in 6.1c.

The necessary amount to make both side agree has been entered on RHS(CR) of the account. It is marked **Balance Carried Down**. (This will be abbreviated to Bal C/D from now on.) Both sides are added up and the total on each side is double underlined and a pounds sign (£) placed in front. A (£) is the usual accounting convention to draw attention to a total of, as opposed to an entry in, an account.

Now by this stage we appear to have done two things "wrong".

First we have made a RHS(CR) entry on an account, i.e. £280 Bal C/D, without a LHS(DR) entry. This violates our rule requiring LHS(DR) entries to equal RHS(CR) entries. (ii) Originally, (6.1b), the account showed H Grove & Co as owing us £280. Now there appears to be nothing owing. But it only appears that there is something wrong because 6.1c does not complete the operation, this is done in 6.1d.

Now there is a LHS(DR) entry. It is marked Bal B/D, which is short for **Balance Brought Down**. This LHS(DR) also leaves us with the correct amount owing, i.e. £280. We would talk in everyday speach of "owing the balance of the account". To be absolutely accurate we should describe the balance with an additional piece of information. What does, say, "A balance of £500" mean? Does the firm owe, or is it owed, £500? Of course this depends on whether we have a LHS(DR) or RHS(CR) balance. The rule is to describe the balance by referring to the larger side of the account.

The balance in 6.1d, is a Debit Balance, the debit side is greater than the credit side. You should get used to describing balances properly. Never say ". . . a balance of . . .", say ". . . a debit balance of . . .", or ". . . a credit balance of . . .".

In Exhibit 6.2 there are illustrations of the balancing of accounts containing different numbers of entries. Dates, although normally required, are omitted. Each will now be considered in turn.

6.2a. The purpose of balancing is to show the account's balance in a single figure. In this example there is only a single figure so we treat the account as balanced. Leave it alone!

6.2b. The balance is Nil. So turn each side into a total by entering £ signs, and ruling off.

6.2c. Here too there is a nil balance on the account. But as there are two items on one side we do not have two totals. We must add both sides, using £ signs and double lines to indicate totals.

6.2d. The procedure here is the same as shown in full in 6.1.

6.2e. Here the three original entries are all on one side, in this case the Debit side. This account has to be balanced. Enter the total of the three items as Bal C/D, total both sides, enter £ signs, rule off, and enter Bal B/D.

This list really covers all the different combinations of entry you will meet. Even in the smallest concern it is desirable, in larger firms essential, to balance every month. What has been described so far is the first step.

EXHIBIT

6-2-a.

DR					NAME						CR
JAN	12	SALES		190	–						

6-2-b.

					NAME						
JAN	12	SALES	£190	–	JAN	29	CASH		£190	–

6-2-c

					NAME						
JAN	12	SALES		190	–	JAN	21	RETURNS		45	–
							29	CASH		145	–
			£190	–					£190	–

6-2-d

					NAME						
JAN	12	SALES		190	–	JAN	20	RETURNS		35	–
						JAN	31	BALANCE C/D		155	–
			£190	–					£190	–
JAN	31	BALANCE B/D.	155	–						

6-2-e.

					NAME						
JAN	12	SALES		190	–	JAN	31	BALANCE C/D		335	–
	16	"		65	–						
	24	"		80	–						
			£335	–					£335	–
JAN	31	BALANCE B/D	335	–						

36

Having balanced each account we take a separate sheet of paper and list all the accounts, putting Debit Balances in a column on the LHS and Credit Balances on the RHS. We have recorded both aspects of every transaction. This has resulted in a Debit (LHS) and Credit (RHS) entry for each item. It follows from this that when we have finished balancing:

Total Debit Balances = Total Credit Balances

Perhaps the "equals" is a little premature. "Should equal" might be better. Let us look at the whole process beginning with the following transactions:

19x1	Jan 1	Commenced business with £10,000 in bank.
	5	Paid rent by cheque £200.
	6	Bought fixture and fittings. Paid by cheque £300.
	14	Cashed cheque £400.
	15	Bought goods for cash £100.
	17	Bought goods on credit from S Robinson, £700.
	20	Cash sales £40.
	29	Sold goods on credit to U Zurper, £600.
		(VAT is ignored in this example)

You may care to enter these transactions in accounts, and then complete the balancing. Exhibit 6.3 shows the result. The next step is to list the balances:

	Debit(LHS) £	Credit(RHS) £
Bank	9,100	
Cash	340	
Capital Account		10,000
Rent	200	
Fixtures and Fittings	300	
Purchases	800	
Sales		640
Debtors	600	
Creditors		700
	£11,340	£11,340

(Individual debtors and creditors are not shown and totals for each category are given instead.)

You will see from this that the agreement does take place. This list of balances is not part of the double-entry system. We have written "Bank 9,100". This is not a Debit(LHS) entry requiring a

EXHIBIT 6.3

DR							CAPITAL ACCOUNT		CR
					JAN	1	BANK	10,000	–

BANK

JAN	1	CAPITAL ACCOUNT	10000	–	JAN	5	RENT	200	–
						6	FIX.& FIT.	300	–
						14	CASH	400	–

CASH

JAN	14	BANK	400	–	JAN	15	PURCHASES	100	–
	20	SALES	40	–					

RENT

JAN	5	BANK	200	–					

FIXTURES & FITTINGS

JAN	6	BANK	300	–					

DR			PURCHASES							CR
JAN	15	CASH	100	–						
	17	S. ROBINSON	700	–						
				SALES						
					JAN	20	CASH		40	–
						29	U. ZURPER		600	–
				S. ROBINSON						
					JAN	17	PURCHASES		700	–
				U. ZURPER						
JAN	29	SALES	600	–						
			(EXHIBIT 6.3 – PAGE 2)							

Credit(RHS) entry in some other account. All we have done is copied out the ledger balances. Remember that, the various Journals were not actually part of the accounts either.

Accountants call this list a **trial balance**. You would be well advised to file it away, as it could be helpful if any queries arose later. So, in accord with the general rule that everything should be dated, you should set it out as

Trial Balance at (date)

So far everything has gone well; we have entered transactions, balanced the accounts, and have a trial balance that agrees. But suppose it doesn't agree? Then we have done something wrong and we must set about finding out what and then setting it right. The error may have taken place at any one (or more) of these steps:

1. Entering in the ledger.
2. Balancing the accounts.
3. Writing out the trial balance.

In looking for an error it is better to work backwards from the trial balance.

First check the addition of the trial balance. It is terrible to spend hours looking for an error that doesn't really exist! Then check that the ledger balances on the trial balance are correct. Not only that they are the correct amounts. Are they on the right side of the trial balance? Have any been left out altogether? Once you are satisfied that the ledger and trial balance agree you can proceed to the next step.

Second, check the balancing of the ledger account. Exhibit 6.4 shows four typical balancing errors.

6.4a. Wrong addition—the debits total £1,200 and the balance should be £1,000. If this is the only error the debit side of the trial balance will be £100 less than the credit side. So check all additions.

6.4b. Balance not brought down—this looks like a nil balance, and will cause the debit side of the trial balance to be £1,000 less than the credit side.

6.4c. Balance brought down on wrong side—this causes an error of twice the amount of the balance. In this case the debit side of the trial balance will be £2,000 less than the credit side.

6.4d. Total brought down—it may seem surprising but this is a very easy mistake to make, and also easily overlooked when checking. In the trial balance here the debit side will be £200 more than the credit side. If, after finding any mistakes in balancing the trial balance still disagrees we must move on to the final step.

Third, check the ledgers and journals. Check the casts in all four

EXHIBIT
6·4·a

DR			NAME						CR
JAN	5	SALES	100	–	JAN	11	CASH	200	–
	20	"	700	–		31	BALANCE C/D	900	–
	30	"	400	–					
			£1,100	–				£1,100	–
JAN	31	BALANCE B/D	900	–					

6-4·b.

			NAME						
JAN	5	SALES	100	–	JAN	11	CASH	200	–
	20	"	700	–		31	BALANCE C/D	1,000	–
	30	"	400	–					
			£1,200	–				£1,200	–

6·4·C

			NAME						
JAN	5	SALES	100	–	JAN	11	CASH	200	–
	20		700	–		31	BALANCE C/D	1,000	–
	30		400	–					
			£1,200					£1,200	–
					JAN	31	BALANCE B/D	£1,000	

6·4·C

			NAME						
JAN	5	SALES	100	–	JAN	11	CASH	200	–
	20		700	–		31	BALANCE C/D.	1,000	
	30		400	–					
			£1,200	–				£1200	
JAN	31	BALANCE B/D.	£1,200						

journals—don't forget the Returns journals. Then check every transaction, putting a pencil tick in the Folio column against both entries for each transaction. At the end any unticked item in the ledgers is probably there by mistake. Alternatively you may find out what is wrong before you have been all through the transactions. In either case re-balance the altered account and adjust the trial balance.

The types of error are too numerous to detail in the way we did for balancing. They will soon become apparent to you when you have to work on a trial balance which does not agree.

To close our consideration of trial balances it is important to realise that agreement does not show that our accounts are correct. Consider these examples:

(i) A charge for rent is entered on the debit side of Wages account.
(ii) Cash received from A Customer was entered on the debit side of An Other-Customer's account.
(iii) A transaction is omitted entirely from the books.
(iv) A transaction was entered correctly, and then entered correctly a second time.

None of these errors will cause a disagreement in the trial balance. That being so you must remember that a trial balance is only a partial check. There could still be some errors in the ledger. The trial balance is mainly a check upon the arithmetical accuracy of the books.

7. HOW MUCH PROFIT?

For the purposes of this chapter we shall be using the accounts of Exhibit 6.3. It gives a very simple example it is true, but it is sufficient for initial explanation. Remember the first step in calculating profit is to balance the accounts and agree a trial balance.

To begin with let us consider how we are going to calculate profit. It will be done in two stages, and first we shall calculate our profit on trading.

We buy at one price and sell at another. Sometimes this is quite clearly seen, as in the retail trade, but it is just as true of manufacturing even if not quite so apparent.

If we take:

	Selling price of goods sold
less	Cost price of goods sold
we get	**Trading Profit**

We can find the first figure quite easily, it is the balance of the Sales account. We have not been paid for all we have sold but this merely means that we temporarily hold some of our assets as "Debtors" rather than "Cash".

The cost price presents more difficulties. How about £800? This would only be correct if all the goods had been sold. With sales in our example of £640 there would be a loss of £800 − £640 = £160. But the question posed is what is the cost of goods sold. We shall have to value all purchases remaining in stock. Stocktaking is not too difficult in practice. A list can be made of items, the price paid found from the invoice, and the total value of stock calculated. In this example let us assume that a little less than half of the stock has been sold and stocktaking results in a figure of £450 for goods in hand. A small calculation shows:

		£
	Purchases	800
less	Stock	450
equals	Cost-of-Sales (COS)	£350

We are now in a position to calculate our trading profit:

	£
Sales	640
COS	350
Trading Profit	£290

The next step is to calculate final profit. COS is an expense of trading but there are other expenses involved in running the business. We must do another calculation:

	Trading Profit
less	Expenses
leaves	**Final Profit**

In the example of Exhibit 6.3 there is only one expense—Rent. Our calculation now becomes:

	£
	£
Trading Profit	290
Expenses	200
Final Profit	£ 90

What we have to do is to complete what is usually known as the **Trading and Profit and Loss Account (P & L Account)**. We are going to do it by transferring balances from the accounts to the P & L Account. This is an Account, and is subject to normal book-keeping rules. Thus a debit (LHS) entry on P & L Account requires a credit (RHS) entry on some other account.

Exhibit 7.1 shows the accounts of Exhibit 6.3 balanced and ready for the preparation of the P & L Account. A pro forma account appears below:

TRADING AND PROFIT & LOSS ACCOUNT

DEBIT (LHS)   FOR YEAR ENDING (DATE)   CREDIT (RHS)

	£		£
PURCHASES		SALES	
LESS STOCK			
COST-OF-SALES			
TRADING PROFIT C/D	£		£
EXPENSES		TRADING PROFIT B/D	
„ SHOWN		(OTHER REVENUE)	
„ INDIVIDUALLY			
„			
„			
FINAL PROFIT	£		£

It is impossible to think of a business that would not be able to produce a P & L Account in this form, so this pro forma may be taken as a standard form. We shall now consider how it is to be used.

44

The main revenue of any firm will be its Sales, so we enter the balance of the Sales account, £640. This is a credit (RHS) entry. In the Sales account we make the debit (LHS) entry. We have, in effect, transferred the credit balance of £640 in Sales account to the P & L Account. There is now no balance on Sales account and it may be ruled off.

In the same way the Purchases account debit balance of £800 is transferred.

The calculation of the stock figures has already been described. To get this into the P & L Account requires two entries.

Debit (LHS) Purchasing account, and credit (RHS) P & L Account, with the value of the stock.

The first entry leaves a balance on Purchases account equal to the amount of stock being carried forward for use next year.

The credit (RHS) entry on the P & L Account is made in an unusual way. The instruction "Credit such-and-such an account" requires some amount to be added to the credit (RHS) side of the account. But here the sum has been deducted from the debit (LHS) side. Rather like the rule for equations: "Change the side, change the sign".

So the entry "Stock £450" is a credit (RHS) entry, appearing as a deduction on the debit (LHS).

The Cost-of-Sales is obtained by arithmetic, not by accounting posting and there is no corresponding credit entry.

The sales of the firm will normally exceed the cost and so there will be a credit balance. This is the amount of trading profit and, in the normal manner of balancing, should be carried down to the second part of the P & L Account.

This second part consists almost entirely of Expenses. In our example there is only one expense, Rent, and this is transferred by the usual entries. On the credit (RHS) side is included other revenue. The vast majority of revenue will be from sales but there may be other small items to include. Some suppliers may have allowed cash discount and there will be a credit (RHS) balance on Discount Received account. If the firm has sub-let part of its premises there will be a Rent Receivable account with a credit (RHS) balance. (Rent Receivable is used to distinguish this from the other Rent account which is an expense.)

Again, the revenue side, credit (RHS), should exceed the cost side, debit (LHS), and the credit balance represents final profit. The entry on the P & L Account is treated as a debit (LHS) entry. A credit (RHS) entry is made on the Capital account. The profit made by the firm belongs to the owner just as much as does the original investment. And so it is correct that the total of the Capital account should be increased by the amount of profit.

However the firm's costs may exceed its revenues. It is unlikely,

EXHIBIT 7·1

DR							CAPITAL ACCOUNT			CR
					JAN	1	BANK		10,000	

BANK

JAN	1	CAPITAL ACCOUNT	10,000	–	JAN	5	RENT		200	–
						6	FIX.& FIT.		300	–
						14	CASH		400	–
						31	BALANCE C/D		9,100	–
			£10,000						£10,000	–
JAN	31	BALANCE B/D	9,100							

CASH

JAN	14	BANK	400	–	JAN	15	PURCHASES		100	–
	20	SALES	40	–		31	BALANCE C/D		340	–
			£440	–					£440	
JAN	31	BALANCE B/D	340	–						

RENT

JAN	5	BANK	200	–						

FIXTURES & FITTINGS

JAN	6	BANK	300	–						

DR.			PURCHASES							CR
JAN	15	CASH	100	–	JAN	31	BALANCE C/D		800	–
	17	S. ROBINSON	700	–						
			£800						£800	–
JAN	31	BALANCE B/D	800							

			SALES							
JAN	31	BALANCE C/D	640	–	JAN	20	CASH		40	–
						29	U. ZURPER		£600	–
			£640	–					£640	–
					JAN	31	BALANCE B/D		640	–

			S. ROBINSON							
					JAN	17	PURCHASES		700	–

			U. ZURPER							
JAN	29	SALES	600	–						
		(EXHIBIT 7.1 PAGE 2)								

although not impossible, that there will be a **Trading Loss**. But it is possible that a trading profit could be turned into a **Final Loss**. In that case there will be a debit (LHS) balance on P & L Account. This is transferred by means of a credit (RHS) entry on P & L Account and a debit (LHS) entry on Capital account. The owner's Capital account is reduced by the amount of the loss.

The reader is advised to open the accounts of Exhibit 7.1 and draw up a pro forma P & L Account. By following through the text both the accounts and the P & L Account can be completed. The completed P & L Account is given below:

TRADING AND PROFIT & LOSS ACCOUNT
FOR PERIOD ENDING 31st Jan 19x1

	£		£
Purchases	800	Sales	640
less Stock	450		
Cost-of-Sales	350		
Trading Profit C/D	290		
	£640		£640
Rent	200	Trading Profit B/D	290
Final Profit	90		
	£209		£290

Note "Final Profit" is a debit (LHS) entry, the credit (RHS) entry is on Capital account.

It is now possible to prepare a trial balance, consisting of those balances in the ledger after the P & L Account is completed.

Trial Balance as at 31st Jan 19x1

	DR	CR
Capital Account		10,090
Bank	9,100	
Cash	340	
Fixtures & Fittings	300	
Purchases	450	
Creditor		700
Debtor	600	
	£10,790	£10,790

At this stage we are ready to prepare the **Balance Sheet** at the year-end. In reality this is merely the trial balance re-written in a specific order. All the items that remain in the books fall into one of four categories. These are **Fixed Assets, Current Assets, Liabilities** and **Owner's Investment**.

Fixed Assets are those purchased for use within the business, in our case Fixtures and Fittings.

Current Assets are those constantly changing and all connected with goods and sales. For all firms this means Stock, Debtors and Cash. These always appear in this order.

Liabilities are amounts owed to persons outside the firm. In this example there is one creditor.

Owner's Investment is the balance on Capital account after profit/loss is added/deducted. This is also equal to all Assets minus Liabilities.

The balance sheet is conveniently prepared in this form.

	Fixed Assets
plus	Current Assets
	Total Assets
less	Liabilities
	Owner's Investment

This has been followed in setting the Balance Sheet of our fictitious firm. The balance on Purchases account appears as Stock. All figures from the trial balance have been used, and the figure of Owner's Investment agrees with that on the Capital account.

Balance Sheet as at 31st Jan 19x1

	£	£
Fixed Assets		
Fixtures and Fittings		300
Current Assets		
Stock	450	
Debtors	600	
Bank	9,100	
Cash	340	10,490
Total Assets		10,790
Liabilities		
Creditors		700
Owner's Investment		£10,090

The whole process of accounting has now been carried through from the original opening of accounts to the preparation of the **Final Accounts**.

(The Profit and Loss Account and the Balance Sheet together are referred to as the Final Accounts.) Book-keeping summaries have been included, as necessary, at the end of each chapter. These, together with the entries to calculate profit or loss, constitute a full set of posting instructions for all transactions likely to be met in the normal course of business. But before we go on to this there are two more problems to consider, and the first is that of **depreciation**.

Much of the confusion over depreciation springs from the fact that the accounting definition of depreciation is a different one to that in everyday use.

Let us assume a motorist paid £5,000 for a new car. In one year he found its second-hand value had fallen to £3,500. He would calculate his depreciation so:

Value new	5,000
Value now	3,250
Fall in value	£1,750 = Depreciation

Depreciation for a period, as generally defined, is the fall in value over that period. But this is not what accountants mean.

Suppose a firm buys the car instead of an individual. There is now an Asset account (Motor Cars) with a debit (LHS) balance of £5,000. The car is expected to last for three years, at the end of which time it will be traded-in for £500.

If you refer to the Final Accounts we have prepared you will see that Assets (in that case Fixtures and Fittings) are not deducted from the final profit figure. This is because Assets are not regarded initially as a cost. But as they wear out, which they do in the service of the business, some part of their cost must be charged annually to profit. It is this charge which accountants know as depreciation. Consider the example of the car already mentioned, and do a little sum:

	£
Cost	5,000
Scrap Value	500
Net Cost to Firm	£4,500
Life	3 years
Net Cost per annum	£4,500 ÷ 3 = £1,500

Vehicles have trade-in values but many other assets can be sold for scrap prices at the end of their useful life. Because of this it is usual to use "scrap value" for all assets.

It is logical to charge the cost of an asset in an orderly fashion over the whole of its useful life. The calculation is simple:

$$\frac{\text{Cost less Estimated Scrap Value}}{\text{divided by Estimated Life in Years}}$$

This gives the "**Annual Depreciation Charge**". This is the amount to include with other expenses. A separate charge must be calculated for each asset. The entry in the Profit and Loss Account will be balanced by a credit (RHS) entry in the Asset account. Each year the profit will be reduced by an appropriate part of the assets value, and by the time it is worn out the balance of the asset account will be nil, or the scrap value if there is one.

Notice again the car example. The layman's estimated market value at the end of the first year is £3,250. Let us assume that this estimate is correct. Our method gives us a different "value":

	£
Cost	5,000
Depreciation for year	1,500
	£3,500

This difference often puzzles people but there is a straightforward explanation.

Laymen's depreciation is based on the value of the asset at any given time, in this case the year-end.

Accountants' depreciation is a consistent charge being made each year.

Accountants' depreciation is not an attempt to fix the value of an asset at the end of each year. It is a system to transfer, in an orderly manner, the value of an asset so that its cost is deducted from profit over its life-time. This is referred to as "**writing-off**" the cost of the asset which is shorthand for "**writing-off against profit**".

Where there are several asset accounts "depreciation" will consist of several separate figures. It is sometimes convenient to use a single depreciation account.

The entries will then be:

Debit (LHS) Depreciation account
Credit (RHS) Individual Asset account
Amount: depreciation charge for individual asset

Eventually all individual assets will have been charged and the debit balance on Depreciation account will be the total charge for the year, which can be transferred as a single figure to the P & L Account.

The second problem refers to expenses. The profit for any accounting year is the revenue of that year less the expenses of that year. But Expense accounts may well include items for other years.

Using the example of this chapter let us suppose that the £200 posted to the Rent account represented £150 for the current year and £50 for the next.

In the bottom part of P & L Account the entries will look like this:

P & L Account—extract

	£		£
Rent	150	Trading Profit B/D	290
Final Profit	140		
	£290		£290

This is quite logical; only the expense (rent) for the year is included. Let us see how this will appear in the Rent account itself. There is a debit (LHS) entry in the P & L Account so there must be a credit (RHS) entry in the Rent account.

Rent

		£			£
Jan 5	Bank	200	Jan 31	P & L	150
				Balance C/D	50
		£200			£200
Jan 31	Balance B/D	50			

This balance is treated in the same way as all other balances, that is it is included in the balance sheet. As it is a debit balance it is treated as a current asset, being included as an "**Unexpired Expense**". This is quite logical as the firm has the right to occupy premises for some time in the future, for no further payment. At the same time the profit figure has been increased to take this into consideration.

It is also possible to think of cases where expenses for the year are unpaid, and so do not appear in the expense account. Let us suppose that rent had been fixed at £240 per annum, and that the premises had been occupied for the whole of the year.

The debit balance on Rent account is £200, but we must transfer the charge for the whole year. The extract from the P & L Account and the complete Rent account shown below should enable you to understand the method.

P & L Account—extract

	£		£
Rent	240	Trading Profit B/D	290
Final Profit	50		
	£290		£290

Rent

Jan 5	Bank	200	Jan 31	P & L	240
Jan 31	Balance C/D	40			
		£240			£240
			Jan 31	Balance B/D	40

Here rent will appear as a liability in the balance sheet and be included in the Liabilities section as an Accrued Expense.

We can now set out in full the procedure for completing the Final Accounts.

1. Enter all transactions in the accounts, which have then to be balanced.
2. Prepare a trial balance, which it is convenient to refer to as the Closing Trial Balance. You must not proceed until this trial balance agrees.
3. Value all your stock at cost price. Where prices have varied over the accounting period some difficulty may be experienced, and in such cases judgment must be used to arrive at a "reasonable" value. But remember you are looking for reasonable cost prices, selling prices are irrelevant. The stock figure is used in calculating the Cost-of-Sales and appears eventually in the balance sheet.
4. Calculate depreciation charges on all assets:

Side	Account	Amount
Debit Credit	Depreciation Asset	Individual charges
Debit Credit	P & L Depreciation	Total charge

5. Prepare the **P & L** Account:

Side	Account	Amount
Debit Credit	Sales **P & L**	Balance of account
Debit Credit	**P & L** Purchases	Balance of account
Debit Credit	Purchases **P & L***	Value of stock
* Include as deduction from Debit side		

Bring Down Balance: Credit balance = Trading Profit

             or   Debit balance = Trading Loss

Side	Account	Amount
Debit Credit	**P & L** Expense	Amount of each expense for year
Balance: Credit balance = Final Profit Debit P & L Account Credit Capital account		
Balance: Debit balance = Final Loss Debit Capital account Credit P & L Account		

6. Take out a second trial balance. This is called the Opening Trial Balance. The end of one accounting year is the beginning of another, and this trial balance contains all the balances with which we shall open the year.
7. After agreeing the trial balance the Balance Sheet can be prepared and the Final Accounts for the year will be completed. The Balance Sheet is a statement, not an account, and so no book-keeping entries are necessary in the way that they were for the P & L Account.
8. As you go forward to next year the following balances will appear in your books:

Debit balances	Credit balances	Comments
	Capital account	Proprietor's investment
Purchases		Opening stock
Various assets		Cost of each less depreciation
Various customers		Debtors
	Various suppliers	Creditors
Cash		Cash balance in hand
Bank		Bank balance
	or Bank	Bank overdraft

8. COMMERCIAL SYSTEMS

The use of account books by small firms would be both expensive and inconvenient. It is possible to buy pages of ledger paper or journal paper, or any other ruling required, and these may be stored in ordinary lever-arch or box files. Such a system would need a cash book, and also a wages book if there are employees. Probably the cheapest system could be obtained this way, indeed in the very small firm it is possible that the complete accounting system could be kept in A4 folders, all stored in a foolscap box file.

If this is the way adopted two further aspects of the accounting system need to be considered.

First there is the **statement of account**. Normally firms settle their accounts, not on receipt of the invoice, but when the statement is sent at the end of the month. By "statement" we merely mean a copy of their outstanding account. It will show invoice amount, date and reference number if any. The business will probably be receiving statements from its suppliers so the general layout will be quite familiar. However, as payment depends upon customers receiving statements, it is essential that they are sent off without delay. One of the advantages of commercial systems is that statements are produced as a by-product of ledger posting.

Second, there is the matter of **discounts, allowed and received**. When a customer settles and deducts cash discount the entries are:

Entry	Account	Amount
DR/LHS	Cash	Amount received (a)
DR/LHS	Discount Allowed	Discount deducted (b)
CR/RHS		Total of (a) and (b)

The reader should work out the appropriate entries for Discounts Received when paying suppliers.

It will be seen from this that an entry will be needed in one of the discount accounts whenever a payment is made, or a remittance received, unless no discount is involved. This is the same position we found with sales and purchases, far too many entries, and we must reduce this number in a familiar way, something which we could call a Discounts Journal. If a list of all discounts deducted by customers is kept, and is totalled at the end of the month, this total represents the month's Discount Allowed. This amount is then entered, DR/LHS, in Discounts Allowed which is simply one of the many expense accounts. The same procedure for Discounts Received, CR/LHS entry, which is a sort of "income" and appears in the Final Accounts as such.

The matter of discounts has been left until now because some of the commercial systems have their own way of accommodating discounts.

There are many firms supplying systems. In some cases these are complete, in others you can set up individual sections of which the sales ledger can serve as an example.

The basis of these systems is a peg-board and suitably punched stationery. Exhibit 8.1 shows the **Kalamazoo sales ledger system**. The

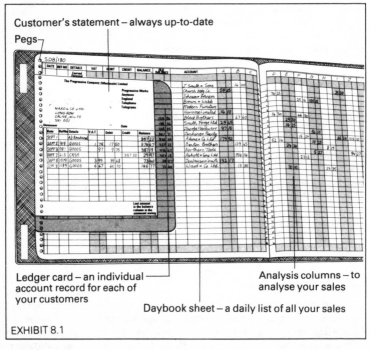

Customer's statement – always up-to-date

Pegs

Ledger card – an individual account record for each of your customers

Analysis columns – to analyse your sales

Daybook sheet – a daily list of all your sales

EXHIBIT 8.1

bottom sheet is the Sales Journal. On to this is placed the ledger card and then the statement. These are positioned, and held firm, by the pegs sticking up on the far left of the binder. No carbon paper is used and all three accounting records, sales journal, sales ledger account and statement, are produced at once.

This basic method is used for all accounting records. A purchase ledger is available with, reading from the top, a cheque, purchase ledger account, and purchases journal all completed from one entry. (Exhibit 8.2.)

Ledger card – an individual account record of each of your suppliers

Journal sheet – a complete list of all your payments

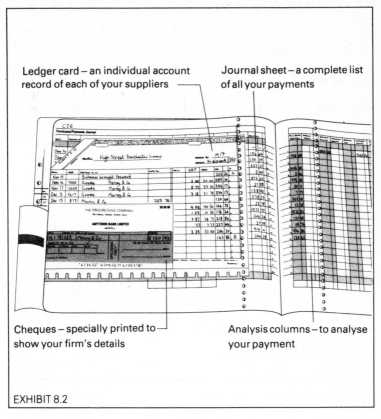

Cheques – specially printed to show your firm's details

Analysis columns – to analyse your payment

EXHIBIT 8.2

Similarly the wages system provides for the main pay record, employee pay slip and tax documents to be prepared in one operation.

Kalamazoo is one of the largest business systems firms in the UK. One advantage of dealing with them is that trained personnel are available to choose a system which best suits the needs of your firm.

You can find the address of the local office from your classified directory. But remember such systems are not necessarily the most economical for you. The "Business Systems" yellow pages will give you the names of other firms who may have something nearer your needs.

However do not overlook the do-it-yourself suggestion at the beginning of this chapter. There is a firm specialising in the supply of a very wide variety of accounting rulings. These vary from the ledger paper introduced in Chapter 1 to analysis paper with sufficient columns to complete the Cash Budget to be discussed in the next chapter. Sold under the trade mark **Bowcourt**, details can be obtained direct from Bowen & Court Ltd, 7 Gardiner Industrial Estate, Kent House Lane, Beckenham, Kent.

So far our consideration has been restricted to financial accounting. Most of this book from here on will be concerned with costing and we must say something about commercial systems available for this purpose also.

Here too Kalamazoo provide systems, such as complete stock control records. A variety of forms, e.g. stores requisitions and stores returns notes, are available. In addition to providing functional systems there are complete schemes for particular industries. Thus a complete financial and costing package is available for small, and jobbing, builders.

As to alternatives and cost the same advice applies here as was given when discussing financial accounting systems.

9. A CASH FORECAST

So far the keeping of accounts has been discussed in terms of knowing, for example, how much our customers owe, our total sales to date, or the cost of the fixed assets being used in the business. All these matters relate to the present or the past. But running a business involves making some sort of statement about the future, and here too accounting has an important part to play.

However many intermediate steps there may be in a business transaction the end result is always a transfer of cash. A firm needs machines, raw materials to be processed on these machines, labour to work the machines. But all of this depends on an adequate supply of cash to pay suppliers, wages and so on. When firms haven't enough cash to meet day-to-day requirements they are said to have a **cash flow problem**. It can cause the downfall of the largest as well as the smallest firm. In an attempt to avoid such problems the prudent managers prepare a **Cash Budget**. You will sometimes see this referred to as a **Cash Flow Analysis**, or a **Cash Flow Statement**.

Normally this is prepared for a year. Our example is for six months, which is sufficient for an example. We shall now work through Exhibit 9.1 line by line. The object of the whole operation is to include in the Cash Budget every receipt and item of expenditure during the month in which it will be received or paid. It will then be possible to say how much cash the firm has at various times throughout the budget period. After seeing how the budget is put together we shall consider its various uses.

Opening Balance (A)

This should include all cash and bank balances. It is unlikely that there will be any amounts on deposit but if there are, and they are readily available, these funds should be included.

It cannot be over emphasised that a casual attitude to the distinction between the firm's cash and the owner's cash can be disasterous. It is true that the proprietor "owns" all the firms resources but discovering the true profitability of the firm depends on a separation of the firm's and its owner's resources.

This is not to suggest that the owner cannot draw out as he pleases. It simply means that every transaction between firm and owner must be recorded in the firm's accounts.

EXHIBIT 9.1

CASH BUDGET

198 —		JANUARY	FEBRUARY	MARCH	APRIL	MAY	JUNE	
OPENING BALANCE	(A)	£100	£3530	£6720	£70%	£3360	£6330	
RECEIPTS.								
CASH SALES		500	500	500	500	500	500	
DEBTORS		14,000	14,000	14,000	14,000	14,000	14,000	
CAPITAL ACCOUNT								
OTHER								
TOTAL RECEIPTS	(B)	£14,500	£14500	£14,500	£14,500	£14500	£14,500	
PAYMENTS								
WAGES		4,700	4,700	4,700	4,700	4,700	4,700	
PURCHASES		6000	6000	6000	6000	6000	6000	
POWER/LIGHT/HEAT				1,200			1000	
MOTOR RUNNING		150	200	150	150	420	150	
TELEPHONE/POSTAGE		20	110	20	20	110	20	
CARRIAGE/DELIVERY								
GENERAL EXPENSES		200	200	200	200	200	200	
INSURANCE				670				
RENT				3,800				
RATES				1,650				
REPAIRS & MAINT.			100			100		
V.A.T.				2,900			2900	
FIXED ASSETS								
INTEREST								
LOAN REPAYMENTS								
CAPITAL ACCOUNT								
DRAWINGS								
TOTAL PAYMENTS	(C)	£11,070	£11,310	£21,290	£11,070	£11,530	£14,970	
CLOSING BALANCE								
(A) + (B) − (C)		£3530	£6720	£70%	£3360	£6330	£5860	

Cash Sales

All the budget entries will be estimates. A good estimate depends on
having figures available for previous periods. It follows that if a book-
keeping system is being set up for the firm the first cash budget may
lack something in accuracy.

Remember not to jot down last year's figure without asking yourself if it is likely to hold in the future.

Debtors

We assume that most of your sales are on credit. If you allow 30 days credit the figure included in, say, March will be sales made in February. If your experience shows that 90% of your customers pay within time but 10% take an extra month there is a different calculation. March cash will consist of 90% of February's sales and 10% of January's sales.

Remember to deduct any cash discount you are allowing.

In the example the same sales figure has been used each month but in the real world firm there will almost always be a seasonal element to consider. The figure included should take this into account.

Capital Account

This includes any amount the owner proposes paying in. If an endowment policy is due to mature in six months time and all, or part, is to be invested in the business this will be shown in the budget.

Other

Any item not yet catered for already goes on this line. Examples would be loans to be taken out in the near future or the proposed sale of an asset.

Total Receipts (B)

Self-explanatory but still a figure worth consideration. A firm will only be profitable if it is generating sufficient cash from its sales. If a downward drift appears in these figures it is probably a sign of trouble.

Wages

Estimates should include any wage increases due, or expected to occur during the period. If expansion is being attempted wages of additional labour must be included.

The term "Wages" includes any statutory payments, e.g. NHI, the employer must make.

Purchases

The same considerations apply as to Debtors. If your suppliers allow credit the relevant date is when payment is made. Deduct discounts allowed where appropriate.

Power/Light/Heat

Accounts for electricity and gas are usually made quarterly. The pattern of oil deliveries will be known to the firm. Lighting and heating vary between summer and winter; power costs will vary if output is seasonal. Items are included under the dates of payment.

Motor Runnings

This will include tax, insurance, petrol, oil, service and repairs. The figures used assume servicing in months 2 and 5 and renewing insurance in month 5.

Do not confuse this with the total cost of running vehicles. To arrive at that figure two additions are required, namely wages and accounting depreciation.

Telephone/Postage

Experience will show how much is spent on each. Unless there are large numbers of letters postage stamps must be bought for cash. Use of a franking machine will result in less frequent payments.

The telephone accounts have been included in months 2 and 5.

Carriage/Delivery

This Cash Budget is designed to deal with all possibilities. It may be that a firm does all its deliveries with its own vehicles. In this case there would be no need for a separate Carriage item. But if rail or road services are used then there would be items to include. Remember that with seasonal trading carriage charges will vary seasonally as well.

General Expenses

These are items which do not warrant a separate account. Examples at either end of the scale may be a jar of coffee for morning breaks to a delivery of printed stationery costing well over £100.

In a sense this figure can be used as a cushion to cover smallish, unexpected, items.

Insurance

Obviously the firm will insure premises against fire and other major risks. It may be necessary to insure for public liability, explosion of boilers, plate glass and so on. It is always desirable to consult an expert.

In any event, once the actual insurance is fixed, an annual premium is payable.

Rent

There are many variations in terms of payment. A monthly, quarterly or whatever sum must be included in the budget.

Rates

For business premises rates are usually payable in full or in two instalments. The appropriate amount must be included under the appropriate date(s).

Repairs and Maintenance
Items of this nature may come at irregular intervals. However, many machinery suppliers offer service contracts and the assumption of the example is that the firm has entered into a quarterly contract of this nature.

VAT
Collections are made on a regular basis, by arrangement with Customs and Excise. Generally speaking quarterly collections seem usual.

Fixed Assets
The replacement of a motor vehicle or machine, or the planned purchase of additions, need to be included in the budget.

Interest and Loan Repayments
These may be included separately or as one item. It is important that funds are available to meet these charges. Failure to meet even a repayment instalment may lead to the loss of your whole business.

Capital Account/Drawings
It may be that the owner intends to draw out in lieu of salary, a regular weekly or monthly sum. This must be included under Drawings. If a large withdrawal is planned it should be included in the budget.

Total Payments (C)
If a firm is less profitable than the owner wishes, and there is no scope for increasing sales, the alternative is to reduce costs. A study of Total Payments may help in deciding when and how this may be done.

Closing Balance (A) + (B) − (C)
It is best to comment on this when summing up, which is the process to which we proceed now.

First look carefully at Month 3. Although the cash balance increased considerably over the six months it did not increase consistently. Month 3 contained many once-a-year items such as insurance and rates. Two other quarterly items came together, VAT and telephone. And there was also a large payment for rent. The overdraft is small but advance arrangements should be made. Your bank will not return a cheque for £3,800 because it will leave you £70 overdrawn. But your standing with the bank could well be affected if the account goes over from time to time without anything being said.

The Cash Budget is a planning instrument as much as a simple estimate of the future. Looking at this cash budget we may ask "Can anything be left over until Month 4?" Insurance definitely not, VAT very doubtful. But if rates are due on the 15th final demands probably will not go out in Month 3. As there is usually ten to fourteen days grace there is no reason why this could not be deferred until Month 4. If all else fails take your Cash Budget to your bank and explain.

Second, we can calculate the increase in cash over the period but this is **not** a profit figure. The amount of increase in cash does not represent the profit figure for the period. Loans may have been made or repaid, capital paid in or drawn out, assets purchased or sold. As well as these there is at least one non-cash item to consider. The full adjustment is as follows:

	£	£
Cash Increase		
less Capital paid in		
Loans raised		
Assets sold		
Sub-total		
plus Capital withdrawn		
Loans repaid		
Assets purchased		
Sub-total		
less Depreciation chargeable		
less any other non-cash items		
Final Profit		

It is possible that the profit of a very small or simple business can be calculated direct from the actual cash flows. However it is really better to use the full profit calculations shown earlier.

Third, the Cash Budget can form the basis of a small firm's planning. If the sales figure is growing month by month remember that purchases will need to rise accordingly. All other expenses may increase, even though not pro rata. In the end it may be found that there is insufficient cash to finance the higher level of activity.

If it is proposed to put emphasis on the Cash Budget then it is better to use two columns for each month. In the first goes the planned or estimated figures and in the second goes the actual at the end of each month. This way a close eye can be kept on how reality accords with the plan!

Finally there is the matter of outside finance. If you go to a bank, or any other institution for that matter, precise details of any scheme requiring funds will be needed. The simplest way of providing almost all the figures required is to produce a cash budget.

10. RETAIL MARGINS, CALCULATION AND USE

One of the major problems facing a retailer is to decide the price at which goods should be sold. This has to be considered from three points of view. These are **competition, the cost of goods,** and **operating expenses**.

There is little need to say too much about competition. A retailer must generally match the prices of similar businesses in the locality. Match does not imply exactly the same prices. More, or less, service than the shop down the road can lead to higher or lower prices which will be acceptable to the public. In some cases, ladies fashions for example, the tone of the shop may lead to different price levels. Some of these differences may accompany differences in cost.

The cost of goods for re-sale is usually the largest single cost facing the retailer. It requires special treatment here, and special care on the part of the retailer. (Although the term "retailer" will be used throughout most of what is said applies also to wholesalers.) The cost of the stock may appear to be fixed but it can in fact be varied in two ways, by buying quantities and/or using cheaper sources of supply.

Buying in quantity has advantages and disadvantages as you would expect. There are financial considerations. If you buy three-months supply and have to pay monthly, some cash is tied up for two months. Of course it may be worth it, but only a properly-produced cash forecast will tell you that. You will also be occupying space and if the value of your total stock is increased you may need to increase insurance. Anyway the reduction in cost has to be worth it. Check this too. What looks a reasonable discount on a total may be too small an amount to be worth it.

This book is about accounting, not retailing, but there are aspects of purchasing that are not always appreciated. Perishable does not only refer to food—a greengrocer would not buy enough strawberries to satisfy a year's sales, but what about a sporting goods shop buying a year's supply of skateboards? Or a children's clothes shop buying a year's supply of Womble clothes? Both would find skateboards and Womble outfits "perishable". Few people in the fashion trade would describe their stock as perishable, but just the same it has the attributes of perishability.

The second aspect of cost is source of supply. Dealing with one source regularly may have many advantages. However it is still worth making checks to see whether the same quality can be obtained from another source. The other possibility resolves around the cash versus credit decision. Obtaining credit, particularly if the majority of sales are for cash, is a way of reducing, often considerably, the amount of working capital required. In some cases suppliers may finance nearly all the retailer's stocks. The retailer may not be able to operate without this credit. But this credit need not be "free". There are cash-and-carry wholesalers in many trades now. Their prices are generally below those of retailers providing more service. (Providing credit is a service.) The retailer should always investigate ready cash sources of supply. The saving in cost may be greater than any borrowing necessary, in which case profit is increased. If cash is available to cover purchases then all the cost reduction is a profit.

As an aside it is worth pointing out that having a lot of cash is not necessarily the sign of a well-run business. There should be enough in the bank to meet commitments, as shown by the Cash Budget, plus a margin. The rest should be used to provide more sales and profit for the firm.

Third, we must consider operating expenses. The Cash Budget shown in Chapter 9 refers largely to manufacturers, but it can easily be understood as a retailer's if "purchases" is taken to be of goods for resale. Some of the expense items would not appear in a normal retailer's accounts but this presents no real difficulty to understanding the principle. At the same time there are other important expenses particular to a retailer, for example there are various promotional techniques available such as trading stamps or give away items. These may be "free" to the customer, but they are not "costless" to the retailer. Whether they are included under the heading of advertising or not is immaterial. What is important is that they are recognised as operating expenses.

A second important retail expense is stock-losses. Self-service, with its tempting invitation to pick up items and examine them, leaves the way wide open for people to take goods without paying.

Third, there are price reductions. Various methods connected with marking up are discussed below. Any goods reduced will have previously been marked-up. Reductions will reduce the mark-up or even eliminate it altogether. Drastic reductions will reduce the price to below cost. Rather than get involved in such complicated calculations it is better to calculate the total reduction of retail selling price and treat this as an operating expense. The calculations will go like this:

Expected value of goods to mark down each week at selling price is £150. Experience also shows that the necessary reduction of selling price averages 40%. 40% of £150 = £60 = weekly cost of reductions. Multiplying this by trading weeks per annum will give total reductions as an operating expense.

In order to examine the problems, and calculation, of the mark-up a single example will be used. We shall call our trader Mr. West. He estimates that his next year's trading will produce these results.

West knows, from his Cash Budget, that he has the resources to buy stock at the rate of £10,000 each month. His stock losses will be £100 each week, say, £5,000 per annum. During a week West expects to mark down by 50% stock selling at £60, say, £1,500 per annum. His other operating expenses will amount to £5,000 per month. His sales will be £18,000 per month.

The first thing to do is to set this out as a profit calculation.

West Estimated Trading Results

	£	£
Sales (£18,000 × 12)		216,000
Cost-of-Goods (£10,000 × 12)		120,000
Gross Return		96,000
Operating Expenses		
Stock losses (£100 × 50)	5,000	
Reductions (50% of £60 × 50)	1,500	
Other expenses	60,000	66,500
		£29,500

These Returns are measured in £s; they will now be expressed in relative, i.e. percentage, terms. To distinguish from Returns these will be called Margins.

We can calculate margins in two different ways, by measuring returns against cost price or against selling price.

Most people think of profit in relation to cost:

$$\frac{\text{Net Return}}{\text{Total Cost}} \times 100 = \frac{\text{Net Return}}{\text{Cost-of-Goods} + \text{Operating Expenses}} \times 100$$

$$= \frac{29,500}{120,000 + 66,500} \times 100$$

$$= 15 \cdot 8\%$$

$$= \text{Margin on Cost}$$

(All these calculations are correct to one decimal place.)

But return can also be related to total sales or turnover:

$$\frac{\text{Net Return}}{\text{Sales}} \times 100 = \frac{29,500}{216,000} \times 100$$

$$= 13 \cdot 7\%$$

$$= \text{Margin on Sales}$$

There is no need to discuss the margin on cost, this being the measure understood by most of us. However the margin on sales is a more useful figure. 13·7% means that £13·70 of each £100 taken is West's share of receipts. If everything in the plan materialises, if sales reach the predicted figures, if operating expenses are not higher than planned, and if stock can be purchased at the expected prices, then 13·7% of all cash taken is profit. Each margin on cost will have an appropriate margin on sales. Examples with round figures should make this clearer.

	(1) £	(2) £	(3) £	(4) £
SALES (S)	100,000	100,000	100,000	100,000
COST (C)	80,000	75,000	60,000	50,000
PROFIT (P)	£20,000	£25,000	£40,000	£50,000
Margin on Sales $\frac{P}{S} \times 100$	20%	25%	40%	50%
Margin on Cost $\frac{P}{C} \times 100$	25%	$33\frac{1}{3}\%$	$66\frac{2}{3}\%$	100%

Exhibit 10.1 gives a table of margins on both sales and profit, and can be used for conversion. Thus, if a firm is adding 40% to cost it can be seen that this is 28·5% on sales. Should 40% be a normal mark-up in any trade a retailer will know that approximately £28·50 of every £100 taken will be profit.

Viewed from the other direction we can say that a retailer wanting a return of 15% on sales, i.e. approximately £15 in every £100 to be profit, must mark-up cost by 17·7%. The table may be used in either direction.

Now we turn to the practical problem of calculating selling price. We shall consider this by using the results of Col (1). The shop-keeper is expecting to make a profit of £20,000. When we estimated his costs at £80,000 he obtained a net margin on cost of 25%. The retailer's problem is that the cost of each item of stock is known, but operating expenses for each item are not. Indeed in many cases it is silly to think of "part" of an expense referring to a particular item. How do we divide the rent and rates between individual items? In the case of a grocer how much should be carried by a pound of butter and how much by a frozen chicken? By their relative values? Or, as it is rent, by their relative size? There is no limit to the foolishness we shall find if we go down this path. So we shall move in a different direction.

To the example of Col (1) we shall add another point, that Operating

A	B		A	B
% OF SALES PRICE	% OF COST		% OF SALES PRICE	% OF COST
4.8	5.0		26.0	35.0
5.0	5.3		28.5	40.0
9.0	10.0		30.0	42.9
10.0	11.1		31.0	45.0
11.1	12.5		33.3	50.0
13.0	15.0		35.0	53.9
15.0	17.7		37.5	60.0
16.7	20.0		40.0	66.7
20.0	25.0		41.0	70.0
23.1	30.0		42.8	75.0
25.0	33.3		50.0	100.0

EXHIBIT 10.1

Expenses are £38,000. We can now re-write the results, because we can now calculate the Cost of goods.

	£
Sales	100,000
Cost of goods	42,000
Gross Return	58,000
Operating Expenses	38,000
Net Return	£20,000

We have already found Net Margins; now let us calculate a Gross Margin.

$$\frac{\text{Gross Return}}{\text{Cost of Goods}} \times 100 = \frac{58,000}{42,000}$$

$$= 138\%$$

$$= \text{Gross Margin}$$

The importance of this figure is that if we add 138% to the cost of goods, and if operating expenses are as estimated, and if sales do come to £100,000 we will obtain a net return of £20,000. Notice there is always a relationship between the two net margins, as shown in Exhibit 10.1. There is no such relationship between net and gross margins. The latter depends on the relationship between cost of goods and expenses. You can satisfy yourself as to this by using different goods/expenses, figures in this example. Thus if operating expenses are £25,000 so increasing cost of goods to £55,000, the Gross Margin becomes approximately 82%.

Out of what might seem a welter of figures let us consider three important points.

(i) The retailer needs to estimate his sales, the cost of goods to support these sales, and the operating expenses of the business. From these he can calculate his Net Return.

(ii) By calculating net margin on sales he can calculate day by day the amount of takings that approximates to profit.

(iii) By calculating his gross margin he is able to calculate selling price by reference to the cost of goods only. An alternative name for this margin is Gross Mark-up.

These are simple management guides, but nevertheless very important. There are qualifications. Undoubtedly the estimates will not prove exactly true. Similarly the mark-up is an average only. Different items may, perhaps because of different rates of turnover, carry different margins. But then no businessman expects his forecasts to be 100% accurate. This average mark-up is expected to give a reasonably correct result.

If at any time during the course of a trading period things are not turning out as expected the estimates must be re-done. This will give new targets in keeping with current trading experience.

So far retailing has been considered in terms of the sale of goods. However a high proportion of retailers are engaged in the service trades. Thus launderettes are entirely for service. Others, hairdressing for example, are largely service but make some retail sales. A retail electrician is much nearer the fifty/fifty mark. Quite an amount of new appliances will be sold but there could also be considerable repair work undertaken.

Each of these types will have different accounting requirements. Where a shop does a large and varying service trade its requirements become much more like those of manufacturer. Some solutions to their problems may be found in Chapters 11 and 12.

Finally there are important retailing matters that have not been considered, for example voluntary chains and franchising. They are not left out by chance. Always in the second, and usually in the first, example mentioned accounting help is included as part of the deal.

11. COST OF LABOUR
AND RAW MATERIALS

Used on its own the word "cost" has no meaning.

Total cost means the addition of all costs involved in a job.

Average cost means the statistical cost of one item out of many identical items produced.

Marginal cost means the cost of an additional item.

Direct cost means cost which can be directly related to a product.

Indirect cost means cost which cannot be directly related to a product.

Variable cost means cost that varies with output.

Fixed cost means cost which does not vary with output.

But cost, without an adjective means nothing.

We shall see shortly the importance of efficient estimating and pricing. But in order to do either of these operations we need to know our "costs". We shall be concerned with Direct and Indirect Costs.

Costs which can be directly related to products consist of some of the firm's **labour costs** and nearly all their **raw material costs**. (This would include goods bought for resale in a retail or wholesale business.) It is with these two costs that this chapter is concerned.

Indirect costs which are often, somewhat erroneously, called "overheads" will occupy us in the next chapter.

The individual accounts form the basis of our book-keeping system. The **Job Card** will form the basis of our costing system.

A complete costing system is very complicated but fortunately, in a small firm, such a system is not necessary. The simplified system to be presented should prove adequate for a small business and will probably be some improvement over existing methods. Before commencing on detailed explanations a word of caution is required.

Every business is unique. Each will have its own problems, method of operation, and approach to organisation. It is impossible to cover every possible variation that will be met in the real world. Our example will be based on a firm with the following characteristics.

It is a small manufacturing firm.

In addition to the owner/manager there are twelve to twenty employees. The bulk of these, say ten to sixteen, will be production workers.

The unspecified product is reasonably standard and the firm manufactures batches to order and for stock.

No single order takes longer to complete than one working week. So, at most, work on an order will spread over only two part-weeks.

Even if we could find a hundred firms that fell into this category it is doubtful if any two would be exactly alike. Each would require its own modifications to the system to suit its own needs.

Businessmen should look at their own firms, look at the system, and see how the system can be made to fit the firm. Some adjustments to existing administrative procedures may be possible but beware of trying to make the firm fit the system!

As already indicated the job card is the centre of the system. A separate card should be started for each order and for each batch produced for stock. There will be as many layouts of job cards as there are firms. Exhibit 11.1 shows just one possibility.

It is convenient to give all orders a **job number**. This should help to ensure that nothing is lost. Make out the job card as soon as the order is received and file numerically. If the goods are not ordered write STOCK against the Customer space.

When production is commenced transfer to a **Work-in-Progress file (WIP)**. When completed put into a **delivered file**.

Prominent display of the delivery date on the job card will enable progress chasing in order to meet delivery dates.

An exact description of the product must be given. This shows up the difficulty of covering the requirements of many businesses. In some cases one or two lines will be sufficient; elsewhere more space may be necessary.

We have now reached the **Labour** section. The four columns, besides that for date, are as follows:

Code, to identify the worker.
Hours worked on job, this is best rounded to the nearest half- or quarter-hour.
Wage rate, see below.
Charge is Hours times Rate.

As work is issued the issuer or the processor should record the time on and, as work is returned, off the job. This is entered on the job card. In a small firm elaborate checks on timing should not be necessary.

At the end of the week wages would be paid on the basis of time cards, or some other clocking-in system. The wages of production workers should be calculated together in order that a total be available which relates to work recorded on the job cards. From this the rate to use on job cards can be calculated. The calculation is simple:

$$\frac{\text{Wages before deductions} + \text{Employer's NHI etc.}}{\text{Total hours worked (per clock cards)}}$$

JOB NUMBER		DATE		
CUSTOMER				
DELIVERY DATE				

PRODUCT (S)

LABOUR

DATE	CODE	HOURS × RATE	=	CHARGE
	(A)	**TOTAL LABOUR**	£	_____

MATERIAL

DATE	MATERIAL	QUANTITY × PRICE	=	CHARGE
	(B)	**TOTAL MATERIALS**	£	_____
	(A) + (B)	**DIRECT COST**	£	_____

	INVOICED	
Subtract	DIRECT COST	
Equals	CONTRIBUTION	£ _____

This rate is then entered on the job cards and the charge calculated by multiplying.

The hours on the job cards are totalled.

They will nearly always be less than the clock card total. Odd minutes spent here and there between jobs, short break-downs and so on are bound to happen. This difference represents an overhead expense and will be covered in the next chapter. The calculation is:

(Clock card hours) less (Job card hours) times (Rate) equals (Overhead)

We are now in a position to deal with **materials**. Before considering the detail an important, often imperfectly understood, point must be made.

Suppose a man is in business making garden sheds. He buys the wood for £30, spends £5 on other materials. He then sells the shed for £45. He keeps £10 for himself and buys wood and materials for £35 and so on. This £35 represents his capital. An oversimplified example, but it illustrates the point accurately.

On his last visit to the woodyard he is told "This is the last lot for £30. The next lot that comes in will cost you £40".

The question you should think about before reading on is:

At what price should he sell the next shed?

Let us base one answer on what he had to pay for the wood.

Wood at cost	30
Materials at cost	5
Total Cost	35
Profit	10
Selling price	£45

But this is not right. Out of this he must buy his next supply of materials.

	£
Wood at new cost	40
Materials at new cost	5
Total Cost	£45

If he sells at £45 he will not make any profit at all, his receipts will be needed to provide materials for the next shed. The correct costing appears below:

	£
Wood at Replacement Cost	40
Materials at Cost	5
Total Cost	45
Profit	10
Selling Price	£55

It is the cost of replacing stock, not what was paid for it, which is relevant. Once stock is purchased it becomes part of your resources. If you use part or all of this resource you will have to replace it. Now what is any resource worth to you? If you regularly use material A and its current cost is £20 per ton, what is the value of 5 tons of A, which you purchased at £15 per ton last year? The answer is £20 per ton. The fact that you only paid £15 per ton originally is irrelevant. Even if you are not replacing an item with one exactly like it **current, or replacement, cost** is still relevant. Ask yourself how much your customer would have to pay now for this item. The fact that you have it in stock at a lower price should be your good luck, not his!

We may now return to the job card.

Some form of control over the issue of stores is essential. Large firms use elaborate methods of recording, securing and issuing raw materials. Some form of **Stores Issues Note** is needed. A possible design is shown in Exhibit 11.2, which doubles as a receipt for any materials returned.

STORES   ISSUE/RETURNS NOTE

JOB NUMBER _____ DATE _____

DRAWN/RETURNED BY _____

MATERIAL   QUANTITY

_____   _____

_____   _____

_____   _____

ISSUED/RECEIVED BY   _____

SIGNED _____

There is no space for Price or Charge, these are included in the job card. Periodically information from the stores notes is transferred to the job cards, which must then be priced. And as you will gather from what has been said this could turn out to be easier said than done. Let us consider two possibilities, the Ideal and the Workable.

The Ideal system would require you to obtain a current quotation for each item. Simple to write down, very difficult to do. The object of this book is to give you a quick, but effective, way of obtaining the figures you need. The Ideal method would be too time consuming, and some of the information gathered would be of little value.

The Workable system requires you to divide the types of material into three groups.

(i) Material used in very large quantities. If over, say, 60% of your material costs come from one item it is worth getting a current quote. The 60% is arbitrary; you should fix a figure suitable for your firm.

(ii) Items which form an insignificant part of material cost should be included at invoice price.

(iii) Items between these two extremes must be sub-divided.
    (a) Those used up quickly should be estimated by looking at the last few invoices.
    (b) Slow-moving items are best priced by getting a current quote.

You will see that pricing draws on three sources:

Current quotation	(i) and (iiib)
Invoice price	(ii)
Estimate	(iiia)

At the end of the job there will be totals for Labour (A) and Materials (B). Added together this gives Direct Cost (A + B).

When the goods are invoiced the amount, excluding VAT, is entered on the job card. The amount Invoiced (D) less Direct Cost (A + B) gives **Contribution** (E).

$$(D) - (A + B) = E$$

This is not profit as overheads have still to be met, but it is an important figure to which we shall return in later chapters.

12. OVERHEAD COSTS

The distinction has already been made between Direct and Indirect Costs. Direct costs, wages and materials, have already been dealt with. All the remainder of a firm's costs are indirect. **They are costs which cannot be directly related to a product.**

Rent must be paid if there is to be any production at all. In this sense there is a "rent element" in the cost of every product. But it is not sensible to spend a lot of time deciding how much rent must be charged against each job. So we put rent in the Indirect category, and do not attempt to apportion it.

Among those items which, in book-keeping terms, had debit balances were purchases, expenses and assets. Direct costs were materials used and wages. Materials used are purchases less stock, and wages are an expense. Indirect costs are all costs other than these. So the position may be summarised so:

	Direct Cost	Indirect Cost
Purchases	Purchases less Stock	—
Expenses	Wages	All others
Assets	—	Depreciation

You will see from this that the largest part of our costs will fall into the category of indirect or, as we shall say from now on, **Overhead Costs.** The method of costing we shall apply is to discover as accurately as possible, the direct cost of every job. The difference between selling price and direct cost is the amount that job earns towards overhead costs. That is why it is called a contribution. It is the contribution that job makes to overhead costs.

After the total contributions amount to the whole year's total overheads, all contributions subsequently earned represent **Profit**. A few simple sums should demonstrate this.

	Selling Price	(of job)
less	Direct Cost	(of job)
equals	Contribution	(of job)
	Contributions	(Total)
less	Overhead Cost	(For year)
equals	Profit	

But if Overhead Cost is greater than Contribution then:

		(For year)
less	Overhead Cost	
equals	Contributions	(Total)
	Loss	

Sometimes this relationship is discussed in terms of the **Break-even Point**. If the firm is profitable part-way through the year total contributions to date will equal total overheads for the year. At that time the firm is breaking-even. It has covered all its costs, i.e. direct costs of output and all the year's overheads. From now on all contributions count towards profit. We shall return to the break-even point.

There is one other important point to remember about overheads. This is the distinction between **Fixed** and **Variable Overheads**.

There are some expenses that do not vary with output. A firm must pay rent and rates even if there is nothing being produced or sold.

But carriage or the cost of running your own van for collections or deliveries will vary with activity.

This distinction is important as, during periods of slack trade only variable overheads are saved by a shut down. Every firm will find that its total costs divide into these categories in relatively stable proportions. Let us imagine two firms.

	Firm A	Firm B
Direct Cost	30%	75%
Variable Cost	20%	20%
Fixed Overhead	50%	5%
Total Cost	100%	100%

The figures are rather extreme but help to make the distinction stand out.

If Firm A runs into a slack period even a temporary shut down of the whole firm will leave it with 50% of its total cost to bear. Firm B on the other hand would have to bear a mere 5% of total costs. In general terms the higher the proportion fixed overheads is of total cost the more vulnerable the firm is to fluctuations in business. The owner of a firm should have at least an approximate figure for the fixed/variable proportions of his overheads.

The actual financial accounting for these costs has already been explained. The cost records do not need a double entry. An Overheads Journal is all that is required. Each expense which is not a direct cost will be entered in this Journal. A column will be required for each month and overhead items are entered as they are received. Thus an invoice from the garage would be included in overheads when received.

The fact that payment has not yet been made is no more relevant than this fact was in the case of sales invoices. Where expenses are paid on receipt of a bill, e.g. electricity, without entry in a ledger account the payment is entered in the overheads journal.

In addition the depreciation charge must appear as an overhead. Whether this appears as one figure in Month 1, or as twelve equal amounts over the months of the year will be discussed later.

By now we have arrived at the outline of our costing system. It is:

	Direct Costs	From Job Cards
plus	Overheads	From Overhead Journal
equals	Total Cost	

With some refinements, in the next chapter we will see that keeping these records takes much of the guesswork out of our firm's operations and provides a framework for profitable decision-making.

13. THE COSTING SYSTEM

In the last two chapters the two main components of cost, direct and overhead, were considered. This covered the mechanics of the system, now we must see the best way to use the understanding we have to improve the profitability of the firm.

To save writing the same words over and over again we shall frequently use these abbreviations:

DC   Direct Cost
TC   Total Cost
CO   Contribution to Cost
OC   Overhead Cost
SP   Selling Price

We can use little sums to show the relationships between these quantities, and to replace long sentences.

$$DC + OC = TC$$

$$SP - TC = PROFIT$$

$$SP - DC = CO$$

A little simple algebra (i.e. change the side, change the sign) gives us:

$$DC + OC = TC$$

$$OC = TC - DC$$

Overhead cost is total cost less direct cost.
Similarly:

$$SP - DC = CO$$

$$SP - CO = DC$$

Selling price less contribution is direct cost.

It is often helpful to be able to rearrange terms in order to understand relationships.

The first use is what we may call a **Contribution/Overhead Diagram** (COD for short). Exhibit 13.1 measures £s vertically and Time horizontally. The time scale has twelve divisions marked representing the twelve months of the firm's accounting year.

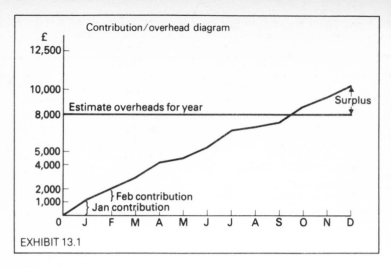

EXHIBIT 13.1

An estimate of total overheads for the year is required. This will be based on previous years figures adjusted for changes in activity. The total for the year is drawn in, as shown in the exhibit.

You should recall that a properly-operated job card system enables you to calculate the monthly total of CO. This is plotted above the Month 1 mark and level with the appropriate £ mark. Join the point to Zero. Month 2 is added to that for Month 1, giving Total CO for the year to date. This point on the £ axis is then plotted against Month 2 and the line from Month 1 extended.

Drawing in this line shows the total CO over the year as it gradually rises to cross the OC line. In our example this happens during Month 10. We have already used the term Break-even Point to describe this situation. From then on the £s gap between the Total CO line and the OC line represents a surplus earned during the year.

Use of "Surplus" rather than "Profit" needs some explanation. The figures used in the COD figure are all approximates. The "Surplus" will not equal "Profit". The latter will be more accurately calculated from the book-keeping records. The COD is an approximation to enable the owner to monitor progress during the year. If the contribution line is rising slowly and sluggishly towards the overheads line something is wrong. More importantly, something needs to be done! Look upon the COD as an early warning system, not a complete method of accounting.

It is important to repeat that the OC line is based on an estimate of current overheads, not just on last year's overheads. However even the most carefully made estimates may be proved wrong by events. Many firms, very large as well as very small, had their estimates badly upset by the increase in oil prices in 1973. If anything happens that affects the firm a new OC line should be drawn at the appropriate, higher, level.

Clearly time is the factor which limits the amount of costing which can be carried out. But in spite of this an endeavour should be made to produce quarterly figures. If CO for the year is going to exceed OC for the year then the same should be true each quarter. Only if trade is seasonal will some periods show OC for the quarter greater than CO.

As the year advances "estimates" of overheads become "actual" overheads and so the figures become more accurate. Thus quarterly figures are more refined, and so more useful, than estimates for the whole year. Incidentally as total overhead cost is charged, and becomes more accurate during the year, the COD can be adjusted accordingly. Raising or lowering the OC line will raise or lower the break-even point.

Further uses of the costing system will be considered in the next chapter. To close now we will consider the relationship of costing and the values of stocks.

In the chapter on book-keeping stock is considered only as the quantity of purchases unsold. This really implies that we are considering a retail business. In the case of a manufacturer the position is more difficult.

The Purchases account will be debited with all items for resale which, in the case of manufacturing, really means raw material. So instead of just saying "Stock" we will have to say "Stock—Raw Materials".

But there will be other items on hand which must be included if our profit figure is to be accurate. To begin with there is bound to be some partially-completed work. The value of this will be considerable and to leave it out of the reckoning will badly understate profit. Valuing it is relatively easy. If the job card system is working properly there will be a file of cards for jobs in progress. Each will include labour and raw material costs to date and from these figures the total direct costs of all work in progress can be calculated. As work is not yet completed we cannot really say that these jobs have made any contribution to fixed cost and it is reasonable to value at direct cost only. Unfinished work is called Work-in-Progress, and the abbreviation WIP is generally recognised.

The third component of stock is finished goods. It is advisable to reduce this to a minimum by the close of the accounting year. If there are orders ready for dispatch and there is no reason for keeping them, i.e. the order specified delivery at some date in the future, dispatch them before closing the books. Whatever is left should be covered by job cards, but it is important to check physically as well.

The valuation of finished goods poses problems. First it must be stated quite emphatically the selling price is not the value to use. The maximum value to use is "Cost". This is in quotes because, of course, we do not know the cost. Every product shares in the various services that are charged together under the heading of overheads. It is not possible to say how much overhead has been "used" by each product, indeed it would be silly to try. However in this case it is reasonable to add a figure for overhead costs to the total of the direct cost involved. What remains to be done is to decide the appropriate rate.

First total direct costs for the year must be calculated. This is total production wages plus raw materials used. Secondly the total of overhead costs must be obtained. If a satisfactory system of book-keeping has been used neither of these tasks should be difficult. Finally the relationship of total direct and total overhead costs should be established, in the following manner:

Total direct costs	40,978
Total overhead costs	61,320
Total Costs	£102,298

Work out the proportion of each category of cost.

$$\text{Direct } \frac{40,978}{102,298} = 0.40$$

$$\text{Overhead } \frac{61,320}{102,298} = 0.60$$

(Both of these calculations have been carried out correct to 2 places of decimals.)

Now work out the relationship of the two categories to each other.
Divide direct cost into overhead cost:

$$\frac{\text{Overhead cost}}{\text{Direct cost}} = \frac{0.60}{0.40} = 1.5$$

We shall call this the **Overhead Cost Rate** (OCR).

This calculation tells us that overhead cost is 1·5 times direct cost or, if you prefer, 150%.

Returning to the job card value of finished goods we can apply the figure to the direct cost total to arrive at an appropriate value. For example:

Direct Cost	3,652	(from job cards)
Overhead Cost		
3,652 × 1·5	5,478	(by calculation)
	£9,130	

Perhaps it is as well to summarise the complete process of stocktaking:

   (i) **Raw Materials.** Physical stocktaking—proceed as in Chapter 7.
  (ii) **WIP.**   Total direct costs from job cards—see Chapter 10.
 (iii) **Finished Goods**
      (a) Total direct cost from job cards.
      (b) Calculate OCR and use it to approximate overhead costs of stock.
      (c) Total direct and overhead cost.

These three totals together give an acceptable value to all types of stock. There is only one final qualification to make. With luck you will never need it!

Suppose a customer goes bankrupt as you are just completing his special order. Because of its "special" nature you are going to have difficulty in selling it. Here are some alternatives.

   (i) You cannot sell it at all so its value as stock is Nil; that is what you include in your valuation. If it does not sell the cost of production is irrelevant.
  (ii) You will not sell it but you can re-work the material. Include it in raw materials, but only at its raw material value. The work you have done is irrelevant.
 (iii) You will sell it, but only as a cut-price job lot. Include it in finished goods at its market value, i.e. selling price.

All this can be summed up in the accountants rule for stock valuation.

Include at the lower of cost or market value.

Except for the last example all stocks are valued at cost. The special case described calls for market value because this is below cost.

It can be argued that, if stock is produced for a definite order, it should be included at contracted selling price. This figure will include the profit which, it can be argued, was "earned" when the goods were completed. This is a good argument although accountants would, with usual caution, reject it. Over this matter you make up your own mind.

14. PRICING AND ESTIMATES

A famous American academic, Joel Dean, once said that pricing was not a one-man operation. "Rather it needs the co-ordination of the cost accountant, industrial engineer, economist, statistician and marketeer."

This book is written for the business man who has to combine these five roles with many others. Dean's comment is reproduced, not to daunt you, but to remind you that you must look at all aspects of the order before pricing it. The list below is of examples, it is not comprehensive. Readers are advised to make up a list applicable to their own business.

(a) Does the order fit into our current production programme or will it cause some disruption?
(b) If the order is for some period ahead will prices of any/all inputs increase? Particular care is needed if delivery will not be completed within one year.
(c) Who is the customer, and what are our relations with him? Is it a firm you have been trying, unsuccessfully, to do business with for years? Would you consider sweetening the price?

Some other aspects of this nature will be considered as this chapter proceeds.

Estimates must be made and agreed with the customer. But estimating is in effect the price-fixing process, so for the rest of this chapter we shall use "Pricing" to cover both tasks.

As a preliminary note remember that a proposal to produce for stock requires an estimate. If you do not do this how do you know you could not buy cheaper outside?

A satisfactory costing system is the basis of efficient pricing. It is not all that is required, as already indicated, but it is an essential element. As nearly as possible we must establish the cost of the product. It is easy enough, if an efficient Job Card system is in operation, to calculate direct cost. The relevant cost in all cases will be replacement cost (see Chapter 10). However it is impossible to attach particular overhead costs to particular products. If you could they would become direct costs. The very reason for our creation of a category of "overheads" was that we had costs we could not allocate directly. But when we are pricing we will need some approximation to total cost. To do this we shall have to employ the device of overhead cost rate (OCR) introduced in the last chapter.

Estimated direct cost plus overhead cost, calculated by OCR, will serve as our approximation for total cost. But this is merely the first step in the pricing process.

Every firm should have a pricing policy or objective. This can take a number of forms. For example it could be a margin of 20% on total cost. Such a calculation is often referred to as a mark-up. From what has been said about overheads it should be clear that this too is an approximation.

It is often found that this figure of cost plus mark-up, simply referred to as "cost-plus", is regarded as a target figure. This is a good analogy. We always shoot to hit a target, sometimes its a bullseye, sometimes an inner or outer. And sometimes we miss altogether. But the pricing objective can be set in other than profit terms.

As most people know the volume of production and sales is important. If overheads are more or less fixed the greater the volume the lower the unit cost. In certain circumstances it may become necessary to estimate to obtain work, in which case covering direct cost and certain overheads alone may have to be acceptable. Looking at a brighter situation, when a firm has passed its break-even point the relevant cost may be direct cost only. This implies not only that there are a number of alternative pricing policies but that policies can, and should, be changed during a year. More will be said about alternative policies later in this chapter.

Let us assume for the moment that a target price has been arrived at. This is not necessarily the selling price. We are considering firms in which the owner is probably estimator and many other things besides. But if there is a separate estimator that person's job is to produce the estimate. The decision as to selling price involves the whole policy of the business. Whatever jobs the owner delegates it does not seem sensible for him to delegate that of final price setting. The estimator provides the information, the owner/manager uses it with other information to set the price.

Most people have heard about "What the market will bear". If the target price is £0·80 a unit and firms in the area are selling the same article at £0·70 a unit some further thought is necessary. If the mark-up is £0·15 per unit the owner must decide whether to reduce profit to obtain a sale. But if the mark-up is £0·05 per unit he cannot quote £0·70 without making a loss.

Alternatively if it is known that the item sells not for £0·80 but for £0·90 the choices are different. Any price between £0·81 and £0·89 will (a) produce more than targeted mark-up and (b) undercut the competition. Exactly where the price is pitched is definitely a policy decision. How low must it be to ensure a competitive advantage? To encourage buyers to switch to you do you need to be 2p, 3p . . . 9p below? Is the quote for an old customer, which involves some considerations of goodwill? Clearly these are matters for the entrepreneur. It is as well to point out that, even if both roles are played by the same person, the two jobs should be tackled separately. Find the target price first then, in the light of policy, fix the selling price. Don't mix the two jobs up.

The final decision has been talked of in terms of price only. But there are other factors to consider. The flow of production is important. New requests for quotations must be examined to see if they will fit in with work already accepted. If not they need never get to the estimates stage. How the firm responds will vary. "We regret that orders already accepted prevent our meeting your delivery date" seems a reasonable response. It lets your customers know that you have a full order book. It also opens the way for them to offer a later date which would fit. Perhaps it is worth mentioning something important, but often over-looked. If your acceptance of an order involves overtime working direct cost will be higher. Something from time and a quarter to double time may have to be paid and this must be allowed for in the labour cost. It doesn't matter if the job is done in normal time or overtime provided the overtime cost is recovered in the price of the job that causes it.

All of these circumstances must be considered but there is another important factor at which we must look in a little more detail. We have already drawn attention to the possibility of greater flexibility in pricing after the break-even point is reached. We shall now look at circumstances where the firm's position is not so happy. To do this we must divide overheads into two parts.

The characteristic of referring to all output rather than specific products is common to all overheads. But there are other important differences between the various overhead costs. This distinction was referred to in Chapter 11, but must now be considered in more detail. Take two examples, Rates and Carriage.

Rates are set by the council. The firm receives a demand, and the amount shown must be paid. This is true whether the firm is working flat out or completely closed. In other words rates are fixed in amount for the year, irrespective of output.

The expense Carriage refers to the cost of delivering goods to customers. Clearly if the factory is closed no goods are being delivered. Expenses for carriage are zero. In other words, unlike rates, carriage does vary with output.

This is an important distinction. Overheads such as rates are Fixed Overheads, those such as carriage are Variable Overheads. The Fixed and Variable categories describe the relationship with output. Rates may alter from year to year, but they remain Fixed in relation to output.

Dividing the list of overheads into the two categories merely requires the question to be asked "Does this expense vary with output?". Of course the items that follow are all examples and not exhaustive.

Fixed	Variable
Rates	Carriage
Rent	Power/Heat/Light
Depreciation	Repairs and maintenance
Insurance	Telephone/Postage
Interest	Non-direct wages

Sometimes it is difficult to put an expense into a category. Motor expenses may refer to the use of a firm's vehicle for collecting raw materials and/or delivering customers' orders. In either case there will be little or no work if there is no output. The driver may be put on short time and money saved on petrol. However the van is licensed and insured, and the depreciation charge must be made. The first expenses are variable, the latter represent a fixed charge. So Motor Expenses are part Fixed Overhead and part Variable Overhead.

With the division complete we can proceed to the next step. We shall use the figures of Chapter 12.

Total direct costs	40,978
Total overhead costs	61,320
Total Cost	£102,298
OCR	1·5

Assume these have been divided.

	£
Variable overheads	18,440
Fixed overheads	42,880
Total overheads	£61,320

OCR was calculated as Total Overheads divided by Direct Costs, in this case 1·5.

We shall now do two similar calculations for variable and fixed overheads, again correct to two decimal places.

$$\frac{\text{Variable overheads}}{\text{Direct cost}} = \frac{18,440}{40,978} = 0·45$$

$$\frac{\text{Fixed overheads}}{\text{Direct cost}} = \frac{42,880}{40,978} = 1·05$$

These rates will be referred to as **Variable Overhead Rate (VOR)** and **Fixed Overhead Rate (FOR)**. Notice that VOR + FOR = OCR:

$$0·45 + 1·05 = 1·5$$

From the examination of overheads an important point arises. It is never worth producing and selling if Direct Cost is not recovered in the price.

But must overheads be recovered? Variable Overhead increases as output increases. A decision to produce increases Variable Overheads by the very definition of "variable".

To sum up so far: a firm will only produce if price at least covers every Direct Cost plus Variable Overheads. Notice the "at least". Direct Cost plus Variable Overhead Cost is not total cost; it does not include Fixed Overheads. Surely Total Cost, which includes Fixed Overheads, is the minimum price we should accept? Well in fact it is not.

Fixed Cost will have to be met even if there is no production. If the price is slightly above Direct Cost plus Variable Overheads this is worth while even if this price is below Total Cost.

If you produce nothing you must meet all Fixed Cost, the total of which represents a loss to the firm.

If we produce goods and sell them at a little more than Direct plus Variable Cost we are able to make some contribution to Fixed Cost. We have reduced the loss by at least some small amount.

It follows that during a slump, in general or peculiar to your trade, Direct Cost plus VOR represents the "cost" figure which must be recovered. Anything above that is worthwhile even if it does not cover "full cost".

Notice that cost is in inverted commas twice. These figures are not True Cost. They are a rough approximation of "cost". They are the best we can get, and are reasonably satisfactory for our purposes.

The calculation requires the VOR figure to be fixed. Then approximate variable cost is:

$$\text{Direct Cost} + (\text{Direct Cost} \times \text{VOR})$$

Many trades are seasonal and have slack periods that are sometimes difficult to fill. Firms sometimes retain production workers on repair and maintenance work. Perhaps machines can be moved, or stores reorganised. But in some cases this is not enough to prevent lay-offs.

But firms can do something to ease conditions by competitive tendering. If the pricing target is changed to "cover variable cost" it may be possible to fill in some at least of the gaps in activity.

Early on in the chapter the need for a pricing objective was emphasised. It was also pointed out that objectives may change. A firm should be aware of outside influences and react by adjusting targets as necessary. Suppose we are dealing with a firm in a reasonably competitive industry with a slack period mid-year. Pricing objectives could vary over the year in this way:

Before break-even	Cost + 20%
Slack period	Variable cost + small profit
After break-even	Cost + 15%

Obviously a regular review of pricing objectives is important.

15. A PLAN FOR THE YEAR

Many people live a hand-to-mouth existence, living from day to day. Unfortunately some firms try and do the same. Some may go on for years and say "It works doesn't it?". It is true that such a firm may survive, but it is as near a certainty as it is possible to get that planning ahead would have resulted in a more profitable business.

About half-way through the year thoughts should be turned to preparing the plans for next year. Last year's results and figures for the current six months will give some indication of trends. You are estimating for next year so using last year's figures would be wrong. But these figures are the basis of the estimate; particularly when viewed in the light of the progress this year.

Some firms are able to manufacture much less than they could sell. Others are able to sell less than they can manufacture. In the first case the firm's manufacturing capacity sets the limit to how much can be sold. In the second case sales potential sets the limit to output.

From these situations we get the term **limiting factor**. All firms have one, and it is important to discover exactly what it is. Let us begin by considering production to be the limiting factor. Here are some examples of detailed reasons for this limitation. The list is not exhaustive.

Production Constraints

(a) The factory premises, including storage space for raw materials and finished goods, are not big enough to allow expanded production.

(b) There is a shortage of raw materials.

(c) There is a shortage of labour, especially likely if some specialised skill is required.

(d) All machines are working to capacity. There is a two-year delivery on new machines.

Of course there are solutions to all these problems:

(a) Rent more space or extend the existing buildings. The first is a short-run the second a long-run solution. Both will add to costs and this must be taken into account in valuing the additional output that would be obtained.

(b) Hunt around for new sources of supply. It may be necessary to send the delivery van on a five-hundred mile round trip. It may mean a higher price for some materials. Or a lower quality resulting in more rejects. All this costs money. Calculate if it is worth it.

(c) Increase wage rate to attract more labour. You will be forced to increase rates of existing staff. Again check if it is worth the cost for the extra output you will get.

(d) Try the second-hand market. Some firms specialise in reconditioning used machines. But if it is second-hand will it be reliable? If a machine breaks down not only are there costs of repairs to meet, there is loss of output and the cost of idle time.

The limiting factor places a constraint upon the firm. Four factors which would set a constraint on production have been listed. Possible ways of loosening the constraints have been set out and this gives rise to three important considerations.

1. **There are short-term and long-term solutions.** Very often the short-term solutions are expensive. Although short-term solutions are often unavoidable the firm should be searching for the more economic long-term solution.

2. **All solutions, short or long-term, involve cost.** Additions to cost need not result in proportionate increases in output. If extra production involves overtime average, cost per unit, usually referred to as unit cost, increases.

Suppose a worker is paid £2·50 per hour for a 40-hour week, during which he produces 200 units. Labour cost per unit is £0·50. If a worker does 4 hours overtime he should produce 20 units. If he is paid £3·75 per hour, i.e. time-and-a-half, his wages for the week will be £100 for normal time and £15 for overtime, totalling £115.

His output will be 200 units in normal time and 20 in overtime, totalling 220 units.

Divide £115 by 220 and the answer is £0·52.

Unit labour cost has gone up by 4%, a not inconsiderable sum.

If production targets can only be met by regular overtime working, overall labour costs are considerably increased. Overtime is an example of a short-term solution as mentioned in (1) above.

3. **A firm that faces a production constraint may seek to reduce or eliminate it. After a certain level potential output may exceed possible sales. The limiting factor now becomes sales.** The firm has simply swapped one constraint for another. So a firm with a production constraint should calculate its sales constraint as well, because this also sets a limit to its level of activity.

So far our description has been mainly in terms of a production constraint, that is with manufacturing as the limiting factor. We shall now consider the construction of a plan in more detail. In order to cover as much ground as possible this will be explained in terms of a sales constraint.

Sales Constraints

Our hypothetical firm has been in operation for some years and manufactures, to order, simple metal components for other manufacturers. This is a reasonably competitive area, but the firm does have a number of old established firms placing regular orders. It has a policy of actively seeking sales, but has never yet reached full manufacturing capacity and has had virtually no recourse to overtime working. The estimate is that output could be increased by nearly 10% before regular overtime would be needed.

Planning starts with the limiting factor, that is the sales constraint. So let us begin by considering what is meant by an increase of 10% in sales.

| Sales last year | £100,000 |
| Sales this year | £110,000 |

This could well be described as a 10% increase in sales.
But suppose this was brought about in the following way:

	Sales in units	Price per unit	Sales revenue
Last year	100,000	£1·00	£100,000
This year	95,650	£1·15	£110,000

This could be described as a $4\frac{1}{2}$% decrease in sales.

The difficulty is that there has been a 10% increase in **sales revenue**, and a $4\frac{1}{2}$% decrease in **sales volume** at one and the same time. During periods of inflation the figures quoted above are, in fact, quite realistic.

There are two points to note. First, "increase in sales" is an ambiguous term. Revenue or Volume? The distinction is important to a trader; it is even more important to a manufacturer. It is so important that a manufacturer should never talk of sales. Rather he should talk of sales-revenue and sales-volume as though each was a single, though hyphenated, word.

The second point is that one of these terms is relevant to production planning, the other is not. If a firm is producing at capacity 100,000 units per annum, and these sell for £1 each, its sales revenue is £100,000. If the price fell to £0·50 per unit capacity would remain 100,000 units, even though revenue fell to £50,000 per annum. When considering production volume, not revenue, is clearly the relevant figure.

Forecasting sales volume is not easy. "Add 10% to last year" will probably only turn out to be true by accident. General economic conditions are important. A buoyant growing economy as we used to have should lead us to suppose that our volume will grow. But there are particular economic conditions as well as general economic conditions.

The general economy may be in decline but the particular area of the economy in which some firms work may be booming. If your firm produces educational or medical equipment it may find life hard, but one in the arms industry may be doing very well. Again unexpected world events may alter prospects overnight. The oil price increase of 1973 is the most striking example in recent years.

We shall just have to assume, for this exercise, that the owners have thought this through to their satisfaction. Now last year's figures must be adjusted to allow for any changes called for.

There are two alternative approaches to this estimation. One, which is totally wrong, is to add or subtract directly from the final total. The correct way is to go through each group of products or, if there are few, each individual product. In deciding how much to adjust each figure further division may be necessary. If different areas of the country have different characteristics it may be necessary to make separate adjustments. Customers may fall into different categories. Wholesalers and Retailers, Local Government and Private Customers, or Home and Export are possible categories which may well move at different rates, or even in totally opposite directions.

It is also desirable that the figures be presented in monthly totals. This is obviously desirable when trade is seasonal, but is helpful in any event.

And so the new aggregate demand figure will be built up systematically. To begin with it will be in terms of volume but this must ultimately be expressed as sales revenue. This too should be done by considering the prices the firm expects to get for each product or group. Bear in mind that the amount received may vary between categories, e.g. wholesalers and retailers.

It is worth considering for a moment large accounts. If one or a small number of customers buy large quantities their part of the sales forecast may require special attention. Obviously if there are any special prices for them this enters into the calculation when changing volume to revenue. But before considering other factors we must decide what constitutes a large account. Generally speaking, if a customer accounts for 10 % or more of sales revenue it would be regarded as a big customer. Some firms are happy with one very big customer taking a very large proportion of output. Some feel safer with a lot of little customers. The choice of policy, the large versus the small choice, depends often upon personal feelings. But often the firm does not get the option anyway!

Let us conclude this chapter with a survey.

We now have a sales forecast which shows:

(a) Sales volume of each product or group on a monthly basis.

(b) Sales revenue for each of these separate figures bases on projected selling prices.

(c) A grand total of sales revenue and sales volume for the year.

This sales forecast is the first step in our plan for the year. The next two chapters show how the plan is completed.

16. COMPLETING THE PLAN

In the last chapter we treated sales as the limiting factor. We shall now go on to produce plans for other aspects of the firm's activities. In doing these we shall assume that no difficulties are discovered which render our sales plan inoperable. It is recognised that, in the real world, such problems arise frequently. But to help readers grasp the underlying method all problems will be put on one side until the end. Having understood a straightforward case attention can then be focused on specific problems.

Having completed a sales plan we must now turn our attention to production. We shall prepare a forecast for direct costs only.

Each month's sales will involve the use of a specific quantity of raw materials. Just as sales were calculated first by volume so too must raw material consumption be expressed as volume. These figures are then converted to value, based on the price expected to rule at the date of purchase.

In the same way labour hours, which could include some overtime, must be calculated. Multiplying by the appropriate wage rate(s) will give direct labour costs.

Raw material and labour together constitute direct cost and so we can move on to the next stage and construct an overheads plan. Here we list all the expenses of the firm that cannot be directly charged. There is no need to spread this out month by month.

Again adding a percentage to last year's total is not satisfactory. The best method is to do a list without amounts, making sure to include all items. Remember that depreciation, as calculated in Chapter 7, is one of the firm's overheads.

When the list is prepared an estimate of the amount of each item should be made. The degree of certainty about the future will vary from item to item. If the firm uses oil for heat and power it will need to take note of the oil companies' statements about future pricing. "It is inevitable that prices will rise in the second half of the year" is the sort of announcement often made. It is a help, but only a little. A rise of $2\frac{1}{2}\%$, 10% or what? Clearly this is important to the firm. Sometimes organisations responsible for post or telephones give undertakings not to seek a price increase for a stated period. All information of this type helps in making reasoned forecasts of particular costs. Not every cost increases exactly at the rate of inflation but it is wise to assume that most will. Goods and services, from stationery to vehicle servicing, can be expected to increase in cost.

It is also important that this estimated increased price be applied to the correct quantity of goods or services. Consider an example.

The cost of vehicle servicing is estimated to have increased by 15% over last year. This cost last year totalled £1,700. Does this mean a cost of £1,955 this year? Only if the £1,700 was for the normal amount of work. Suppose this figure included £900 for work on a special unexpected repair. If this were the case the 15% should be added to £800 (£1,700 − £900). Blindly adding "something" to every figure is not satisfactory.

Finally, on the subject of overheads, another word on depreciation. If it is known that new machinery, vehicle(s), or other assets are being acquired part-way through the year an appropriate adjustment must be made for depreciation.

This leaves us with the cash plan or forecast. This was discussed fully in Chapter 9 and the reader should refer back if necessary. Here only three additional points will be made.

(i) Sales receipts and payments for purchases are included in the month in which payment is received, or remitted, by you. Discounts should be deducted. The sums included should be those actually expected to change hands. Do not ignore discounts you will receive so that they can be a sort of reserve.

(ii) Add a contingency row to the cash forecast shown in Chapter 9. Make a definite reserve for unexpected items. Do not "add a little" to expense estimates and "deduct a little" from revenues, e.g. leaving out discounts to be received. Make a single, reasonably-sized, allowance rather than have a jumble of, largely invisible, adjustments.

(iii) All the items appearing in the Sales Production, and Overheads Plans will find their way into the Cash Forecast with one exception. Depreciation is a non-cash expense. It appears in profit calculations but not in cash transactions.

Before going on to consider how real world problems affect these plans let us review our work so far.

We now have forecasts for Sales, Production, Overheads and Cash. Recognising the difficulty of foreseeing the future with absolute accuracy we realise that we shall not achieve these exact results. Yet, if we have been sensible, as opposed to wishful, in our thinking we shall get somewhere near them. But these plans have another purpose. They represent the best results we can achieve, bearing in mind our limiting factor. So it is not only a plan, it is also a target. If the firm has the resources to obtain this result it should try and do just that. The target aspect of the plan will be taken up again in the next chapter.

Now let us consider the problems that may arise during the course of forecasting. We are still assuming that sales is the limiting factor. Forecasts are produced in the order already described. Here is a selection of difficulties. All major problems are included but the list is not meant to be exhaustive. Some less important, but still troublesome, dilemma may face you. Probably particular industries have their own peculiar difficulties.

(i) The Sales Forecast is completed, but the Production Forecast does not fit. The exact products called for in the Sales Forecast cannot be produced as required. This is a problem of programming production, or production scheduling, which is outside the scope of this book. However, assuming the plans do not fit there are in this, and indeed all other cases, two steps to take.

First see if the difficulty can be overcome. If it is a bottleneck can we obtain another machine and labour to operate it. (Do not forget to add the cost to the appropriate plans!) Could some specific items be produced in advance of requirements? This month's sales need not be this month's output. (Check storage space, insurance, etc and calculate extra cost.)

Secondly if the difficulties cannot be overcome the two plans must be altered. You simply have to juggle them around until they are completely consistent. Bear in mind that as you do this you will probably need to alter the Cash and/or Overhead Forecasts.

(ii) The annual total of the Sales Forecast less that of the Production Forecast gives forecast Gross Profit. If there is no Gross Profit this means that at current prices and costs the firm cannot even cover direct costs. If this is the case and the forecasts are correct, including the arithmetic, the firm is not justified in continuing trading in its present market.

(iii) The example of (ii) is an extreme case. But it is possible that, when we move on to the Overhead Forecast, we shall find that the sales revenue does not cover production cost plus overheads.

In this case the steps are as follows:

First check the Overhead Forecast. Fixed Overheads (see Chapter 14) cannot be altered but economies may be made in Variable Overheads. Be sure that any reductions are possible and genuine. Do not sell a lorry; thus saving depreciation, insurance, tax, and wages; if this means the firm cannot collect and deliver all that is necessary. If the firm finishes up using carriers or hired transport there is no advantage, and an "economy" is not really possible. And make "genuine" alterations. Do not "Knock a few hundred off here and there!". If your original estimates were made carefully they should be allowed to stand.

Secondly check the Production Forecast. Are there any economies to make in raw material cost or usage? Is there a cheaper source of supply; could the product be re-designed a little to reduce materials or labour cost? Remember you are making your plans at least six months in advance. It is true that it is easy to say re-design, though some technical people may throw their hands up in horror at the suggestion. If they were asked to do it by next week, or next month, they would be perfectly justified. But six months gives everyone time to reconsider.

Thirdly check the Sales Forecast for prices. If there is no net profit it means that products are not earning sufficient contribution to cover overheads. If price increases are not expected to lead to decreases in sales an adjustment can be made to sales revenue. But if sales are expected to fall on a price increase both the Sales and Production Forecasts must be adjusted. This possibly means an adjustment to the Overheads Forecast and certainly an adjustment to the Cash Forecast.

(iv) Let us assume that after the first three forecasts are reconciled we find that the Cash Forecast shows insufficient funds. This can take different forms. Thus (a) is an overall cash surplus, but with some periods in deficit, or (b) an overall deficit. Consider each in turn:

(a) This opens two possibilities. First to rearrange payment dates to eliminate the deficit periods. Rates, electricity and telephone bills can be held over until final demands are received. If it can be done without loss of discount and/or goodwill suppliers accounts can be held over. There is nothing wrong in doing this. During periods of crisis very large firms are well known for squeezing the smaller suppliers. But if suitable re-arrangement cannot be made we must look elsewhere for an answer.

This is the second possibility, raising temporary finance. Generally speaking bank overdrafts are looked to for this purpose. An overdraft will be expensive, and cost is based on the balance overdrawn. It may well be that the firm would still wish to re-schedule some payments, postponing them from cash deficit to cash surplus periods. But it should not be forgotten, particularly in a family business, that there may be resources available which are much cheaper than overdrafts. If a member of the family has a significant investment of savings certificates the return today is around 10% per annum. A bank overdraft is in the region of 16% per annum. By cashing the certificates, using the funds in the firm, and then re-purchasing certificates, both family and firm benefit. The individual could earn 13% instead of 10% per annum and the firm pay 13% instead of 16% per annum. Obviously if the sum is very large the possibility of doing this is not great but it should always be considered.

(b) This is a different problem entirely. The cash resources are insufficient to carry on operating at the planned level. Either plans must be scaled down to fit the resources or more funds must be raised to finance the plans. You should already be able to work on the other forecasts without further discussions, but raising further funds needs a little elaboration.

Unlike (a) above, which needed temporary finance, here the need is for permanent capital. Generally speaking temporary finance is more expensive than permanent. It may be possible for a firm to exist on an overdraft for a long time, but it is not desirable. The exact form the financing should take, what advice to seek on fund raising, and similar matters are dealt with in a companion volume in this series, *Finance for small businesses*.

This completes our consideration of the different forecasts and their reconciliation. In the next chapter we can draw together the work of this and the previous chapters.

17. A PROFIT PLAN

We have now considered Sales, Production, Overheads and Cash Plans. What we have done is to complete a large part of a **Budgetary Control System**. Not all small manufacturing firms carry out this operation, partly because it is felt to be too complicated and because it does not seem worth it for small firms. Let us consider these two reasons separately.

The larger the firm the more complicated all accounting systems become. The average text book is written with such large firms in mind and so appears very, very difficult. As well as this these books are written for students who are studying accounting and who already have a considerable background in the subject. So the text assumes the reader has considerable knowledge of accounting already. All this makes budgetary control almost impossible to understand. But sufficient can be explained, free of the more complicated accounting terminology, to enable the small firm to operate such a system. This has been the work of Chapters 9, 15 and 16, and is now to be completed here.

As to the "not worth it" argument, this can be disposed of by remembering that a small firm has to have some idea of what it is doing and where it is going. The author would assert that all businessmen plan ahead. In many cases these plans will be thought out but not put down on paper. All that is suggested now is that these plans be formalised. Already some advantages will be apparent in so doing, not least of which is that the form of the budget is a guide to logical thinking. Subsequently other, quite considerable, advantages should become apparent. That being the case we shall now continue our planning.

The starting point of our plan for next year will be the closing figures of last year. We shall call this year Y, and last year $Y - 1$. Exhibit 17.1 shows abbreviated Final Accounts for last year, Year $Y - 1$. Throughout these examples the thousands are omitted.

Sales being the limiting factor we start with the Sales Budget, and then move on to Production, Overheads and Cash Budget, in that order. Monthly figures are not included, only totals are quoted with any qualification necessary. We assume no inconsistencies between Budgets.

Various adjustments are made for estimated changes in debtors, creditors and stocks.

We have now available to us summarised Sales, Production, Overheads and Cash Budgets. From these we can prepare abbreviated Final Accounts for Year Y in the same form as those for Year $Y - 1$, in Exhibit 17.1. This second set of accounts is shown in Exhibit 17.2.

(i)   *Sales Budget*   Annual sales £119.

(ii)   *Production Budget*   £
             Stock Opening   9   See Balance Sheet
             Purchases   32   Based on Sales Budget
                                     ——
                                     41
             Stock Closing   11   Estimate
                                     ——
                                     30
             Wages   19   Based on Sales Budget
                                     ——
                                     49
                                     ══

(iii)   *Overheads Budget*   Annual total £59.

                   This includes: Interest on loan   £2
                                    Depreciation   £1

(iv) The *Cash Budget* is a slightly longer calculation.

		£	£	
	Cash Balance—Opening		1	Balance Sheet Y − 1
	Sales	119		Sales Budget
(+)	Debtors—Opening	10		Balance Sheet Y − 1
		129		
(−)	Debtors—Closing	13		Estimate
	Receipts from Operations	116	116	
		═══	117	
	Purchases	32		Production Budget
(+)	Creditors—Opening	8		Balance Sheet Y − 1
		40		
(−)	Creditors—Closing	9		Estimate
		31		
	Wages	19		Production Budget
	Direct Costs Paid	50	50	
		══	67	
	Overheads	59		Overheads Budget
(−)	Depreciation	1		Overheads Budget
	Overheads Paid	58	58	
		══	9	
	Loan Repayment		3	From Ledger Account
	Cost Balance—Closing		£6	

EXHIBIT 17.1.

('000 OMITTED) (YEAR Y-1)	£	£
SALES		102
DIRECT COSTS	40	
OVERHEADS	53	93
PROFIT		£ 9
BALANCE SHEET		
FIXED ASSETS	67	
DEPRECIATION	19	48
CURRENT ASSETS		
STOCK	9	
DEBTORS	10	
CASH	1	20
TOTAL ASSETS		68
LIABILITIES		
CREDITORS		8
		£ 60
CAPITAL EMPLOYED		
LOAN		20
OWNER'S CAPITAL	31	
PROFIT	9	40
		£ 60

This is the end product of the process. It is the firm's **Profit Plan**. Sometimes the terms **Budgeted Profit and Loss Account** or **Master Budget** are used. It shows where the firm will be, in capital as well as profit terms, if the estimates are accurate. Complete accuracy is not expected but if the budgets have been prepared carefully, using all the information at the owner's disposal, the actual results should be within reasonable

113

EXHIBIT 17.2

('000 OMITTED) YEAR(Y)	£	£	FIGURES OBTAINED FROM :
SALES		119	SALES BUDGET
DIRECT COST	49		PRODUCTION BUDGET
OVERHEADS	59	108	OVERHEAD BUDGET
PROFIT		£ 11	
BALANCE SHEET			
FIXED ASSETS	67		BALANCE SHEET (Y-1)
DEPRECIATION	20	47	ABOVE + OVERHEAD BUDGET
CURRENT ASSETS			
STOCK	11		PRODUCTION BUDGET
DEBTORS	13		CASH BUDGET
CASH	6	30	CASH BUDGET
TOTAL ASSETS		77	
LIABILITIES			
CREDITORS		9	ESTIMATED
		£ 68	
CAPITAL EMPLOYED			
LOAN	20		BALANCE SHEET (Y-1)
REPAYMENT	3	17	CASH BUDGET
OWNER'S INVESTMENT	40		BALANCE SHEET (Y-1)
PROFIT	11	51	CURRENT CALCULATIONS
		£ 68	

range of the estimate. If at the end of the budgeting process the results are not considered satisfactory then it is back to the beginning! Can sales be increased over the original budget? Direct costs or overheads reduced? Profit Planning does not just tell owners what profits they can expect. It gives them the opportunity to improve profit figures if at all possible.

This completes, with one exception, our consideration of the preparation of budgets. The next chapter will deal with the control aspect of "Budgetary Control". However up to now most of our consideration has been of running costs rather than the costs of capital equipment. Apart from the depreciation charge there has been no examination of capital expenditure. Yet this is an important matter. Firms must replace machinery as it wears out but, perhaps more important, firms hoping to expand must generate sufficient profit and funds to buy extra capital equipment, and plan for its acquisition.

So it is really necessary to add a **Capital Budget** to our list. This will be slightly different from other Budgets for a variety of reasons.

First firms know, with far more certainty, when they are going to need replacements for worn out items. There is less certainty, for example, about next year's sales.

Secondly the time period covered is much longer than other Budgets. Next year a new van, the year after one replacement machine and the year after that another replacement machine. Such three year estimates are quite normal in these circumstances.

Finally there is the problem of additional machinery. If a firm has a Profit Plan which requires a greater productive capacity than at present it will need to plan capital expenditure several, preferably five, years ahead. The first of these years will be incorporated in next year's Budgets and future years added to the end of the **Long Term Capital Budget**, as we had better call it.

These three considerations impart to the Capital Budget its different character to the other Budgets. But remember that new capital equipment has a direct bearing on several different Budgets. The purchase of an additional machine will require entries in four Budgets:

Capital Budget —Cost of purchasing and installing new equipment.
Cash Budget —Payment in appropriate month(s).
Production Budget—Cost of materials and labour.
Overheads Budget —Depreciation charge.

18. MEASURING FINANCIAL PERFORMANCE

As the basis of our planning system we have prepared a series of budgets for the year ahead. These comprise:

Sales Budget
Operating Budget
Overheads Budget
Cash Budget
Short-term Capital Budget
Master Budget

In addition there should be a Long-term Capital Budget covering four or five years.

To complete these budgets is the first essential step, but they are not merely plans. They have an important part to play in controlling the firm's activities, hence the term **Budgetary Control**.

You will recall that Job Cards were first described as a way of gathering cost information. Later it was pointed out that Job Cards could also be used for progress chasing. The art of accounting, particularly for the small firm, is to make one piece of paper do several jobs.

Clearly each budget shows forecasts. Instead of using one column for each month use two, one headed Budgeted and the second Actual. By comparing actual results with the plan the manager(s) can see what is going right and what is going wrong. There are two advantages.

The first is **management by exception**. With a limited number of decision-makers, possibly only one, time must be used effectively. So the only examination needed is of those items which are not on target.

Suppose, for example, that everything was on target except the raw materials forecast, which was much higher in value than budgeted. There are a number of possible reasons for this:

(i) Prices have risen since budgeting.
(ii) More raw material being used for each product than originally estimated because
    (a) the machines produced more defective units;
    (b) labour carelessness wasted material;
    (c) design problems caused wastage.
(iii) Security problems, i.e. pilfering.

117

(iv) Faults in checking delivery, accounting for issues, or other administrative functions.

It is not an easy job to trace the reasons for below-budget performance. Sometimes, as in (i) above, there does not appear to be anything to be done. Usually in the short run there is not, but this should not stop some thought being given to the longer term. There are some steps to be taken in example (i):

(a) Revise selling price.
(b) Look for other sources of supply.
(c) Enquire if there are price advantages in buying in bulk.
(d) See if the product could use another, cheaper material, if only in part.
(e) Check if machines can be adjusted to produce less waste.
(f) Check labour methods as in (e).

It may not be possible to operate (a) and so (b) to (f) must be examined.

Long and difficult though all this may be total work is reduced if only one aspect is under consideration. Management by exception is tremendously important in the small firm, but it depends on satisfactory budgeting being carried out in the first place. If monthly comparison seems too great a burden then quarterly checking should be undertaken. Quarterly is a minimum, monthly is best.

The second importance of budgeting, and the comparison of this with actual, is that preventive action can be taken at an early stage. To revert to the raw material example suppose prices turned out to be 20% up on those budgeted. If no checks were made during the year the owner would simply find that the profit figure was much less than expected. If selling price could be increased the firm would make a lower than possible profit. Early signals that something is wrong can lead to early remedial action.

In summary Budgetary Control allows for management by exception and early remedial action. This facilitates effective management and allows firms to achieve the full potential profitability.

The discussion so far has been in terms of the future and the present. Forecasting for the future enables the firm to monitor its present performance. Now we shall consider the past and show how the analysis of previous results can help us in planning the future. To do this we shall be using the results of Chapter 17. For convenience these are reproduced as Exhibit 18.1. They will be used to examine the financial results and operational performance of the firm. Obviously financial and operational performance are inter-related but, for convenience only, they

EXHIBIT 18.1

('000 OMITTED) YEAR(Y)	£	£	FIGURES OBTAINED FROM :
SALES		119	SALES BUDGET
DIRECT COST	49		PRODUCTION BUDGET
OVERHEADS	59	108	OVERHEAD BUDGET
PROFIT		£ 11	
BALANCE SHEET.			
FIXED ASSETS	67		BALANCE SHEET (Y-1)
DEPRECIATION	20	47	ABOVE + OVERHEAD BUDGET
CURRENT ASSETS.			
STOCK	11		PRODUCTION BUDGET
DEBTORS	13		CASH BUDGET
CASH	6	30	CASH BUDGET
TOTAL ASSETS.		77	
LIABILITIES			
CREDITORS		9	ESTIMATED
		£ 68	
CAPITAL EMPLOYED			
LOAN	20		BALANCE SHEET (Y-1)
REPAYMENT	3	17	CASH BUDGET
OWNER'S INVESTMENT	40		BALANCE SHEET (Y-1)
PROFIT	11	51	CURRENT CALCULATIONS
		£ 68	

will now be considered separately; with the operational aspect postponed to the next chapter.

The purpose of operating a business is to make a profit. The measure of success, or otherwise, is profitability. But there is some ambiguity in "profit" as a measure.

Suppose you are told that the profit of Firm A was £10,000 last year and that for the same period Firm B's profit was £15,000. Can we say, unambiguously, that B is more profitable than A? Not really.

Assume that the owner of A had invested £50,000, and the owner of B had invested £80,000. We are now in a position to do a calculation of Profit over Investment times 100.

$$A \quad \frac{\text{Profit}}{\text{Investment}} \times 100 = \frac{10,000}{50,000} \times 100 = 20\%$$

$$B \quad \frac{\text{Profit}}{\text{Investment}} \times 100 = \frac{15,000}{80,000} \times 100 = 18\tfrac{3}{4}\%$$

We call the percentage figure the **Rate of Profit**. It measures profit in relation to investment. So in this sense the higher the rate of profit the more "profitable" the business. A profitability measure that takes into consideration the investment needed to achieve a given amount of profit is desirable. After all owners, or potential owners, always need to know how much they must invest; not just how much, in pounds and pence, the business earns. So from now on we shall measure profit as a rate rather than an amount.

In practice a firm's success depends on more than profitability alone. It also needs to generate enough cash to meet its day to day obligations to pay workers and suppliers. The phrase "Cash flow problem" is all too well known these days. So we shall measure the firm's success by **Profitability** and **Liquidity**, concentrating at first on figures for the latest year, Year Y.

The first measure is of overall profitability. Omitting thousands as before, the profit earned is £11. How much capital was employed in earning this profit? The total assets employed appear as £77, but from this we must deduct £9 owing to our suppliers. The calculation then becomes:

$$\frac{\text{Profit}}{\text{Capital Employed}} \times 100 = \frac{11}{68} \times 100 = 16.2\%$$

We shall call this **Net Operating Return (NOR)**. All these calculations are best made correct to one place of decimals.

But NOR shows the return earned by the business as a whole. The proprietor will also want to know the rate of earnings on his own investment in the business.

$$\frac{\text{Profit}}{\text{Owner's Investment}} \times 100 = \frac{11}{51} \times 100 = 21.6\%$$

We shall call this **Return on Investment (ROI)**. If there is no borrowed capital NOR and ROI are synonymous.

120

There are a large number of profitability ratios in use and you may well care to consult any of the many textbooks. The two suggested here will normally be sufficient for the purposes of the smaller firm.

When we turn to liquidity considerations we must make a division on the basis of time. Liquidity may be looked at on a Short-term or a Long-term basis. **Short-term liquidity is concerned with the firm's ability to meet current payments. It rests on the concept of Working Capital.**

Every firm must invest in fixed assets. Buildings, machinery, and vehicles, for example. But it must also buy raw materials and pay labour.

This first group is referred to as Fixed Assets. Cash is used to purchase these assets which then remain within the firm.

The second group has totally different characteristics. Here the assets are kept only a short time (materials) or used up at once (labour). These are assets which need to be replenished continuously to enable the firm to continue in operation. So the need is for adequate supplies of such items and sufficient cash to replenish these supplies and meet the cost of labour. This used to be called circulating capital, a good descriptive name, and is now referred to as working capital. It can be seen that having an adequate amount of working capital is as important to a firm as having sufficient fixed assets.

In accounting terms Working Capital is defined as Current Assets less Current Liabilities. In our example for Year Y this is £$(30 - 9) = £21$.

Although this figure is useful it is still better to express it in terms of a ratio.

$$\frac{\text{Current Assets}}{\text{Current Liabilities}} = \frac{30}{9} = 3 \cdot 3$$

We shall call this the **Working Capital Ratio (WCR)**. This figure is always expressed as a decimal.

Although working capital is an important concept and needs to be measured, it is too wide an expression to evaluate the firm's ability to meet immediate commitments. Working capital includes stock, and in our example this consists of raw material, WIP and finished goods. It will take some time to put the raw materials through the production process, turn them into finished goods, sell them (i.e. turn them into debtors), and then collect the cash. So this part of stock, at least, cannot be regarded as available for "immediate" needs. In fact it is usual to eliminate all classes of stock from this calculation using, at the top of the fraction, Current Assets less Stock, or more conveniently Debtors plus Cash.

$$\frac{\text{Debtors} + \text{Cash}}{\text{Current Liabilities}} = \frac{19}{9} = 2 \cdot 1$$

We shall call this **Liquid Capital Ratio (LCR)**.

These two ratios, WCR and LCR, constitute our short-term measures of liquidity and we can now turn our attention to the long-term.

Short-term liquidity sets out to measure the ability of the firm to provide the resources to meet its immediate operational needs. Long-term liquidity measures the firm's ability to provide funds for operations over a longer period.

Most, if not all, firms are unable to provide the resources needed over the whole of the business's life. Nevertheless most wish to keep borrowing to a minimum. The relationship between owner's capital and borrowing is known as **Capital Gearing**. A firm with a high proportion of borrowing is referred to as High Geared, and vice versa. A measure of gearing is easy to construct.

$$\frac{\text{Borrowing}}{\text{Capital Employed}} \times 100 = \frac{17}{68} \times 100 = 25 \cdot 0\%$$

We shall call this the **Capital Gearing Ratio (CGR)**. We have calculated five ratios. (Percentages are not strictly speaking ratios, but the term **Accounting Ratios** is generally applied to all figures calculated in this way.) Before considering their significance you should calculate the corresponding figures for Year $Y - 1$. Ratios for both years are shown in Exhibit 18.2.

The first question many people ask is "What is the right ratio?". The answer is "There isn't a right ratio". Much depends on the type of firm, the industry or trade, and the size of the firm.

Profit rates and liquidity requirements are different in, say, retailing and manufacturing.

The same is true within retailing. Results and requirements differ between a newsagent and a jeweller, and ratios for Tesco will differ from those of a small corner-shop grocer.

It should also be remembered that firms are drastically affected by outside economic climate. A firm may have an NOR of 20% over a number of boom years. During a recession this may fall to 5%. Does this mean the firm's performance is unsatisfactory? If other, similar, firms are making losses the answer, surprising though it may seem at first, is "No".

This refers to profitability, but there are said to be some rules about WCR and LCR. These are by no means accepted by everyone. As one writer says "No good reason for fixing on these numbers seem ever to have been given". So these are stated here without any further argument, for or against.

Adequate working capital is signified when WCR is between 2 and 3. LCR should never fall below 1. Remember that there are some things

FINANCIAL PERFORMANCE RATIOS

		(Y)	(Y−1)
PROFITABILITY			
	NOR	16.2%	15.0%
	ROI	21.6%	22.5%
LIQUIDITY			
	WCR	3.3	2.5
	LCR	2.1	1.4
GEARING			
	CGR	25.0%	33.3%

EXHIBIT 18.2

which do not show up in the accounts. If the bank has sanctioned an overdraft with a limit of £10,000 this is a liquid resource, available for meeting immediate payments and provides working capital. Such matters must be considered; ratios must not be accepted blindly.

As there has been so much criticism of ratios so far you may wonder why the topic is being discussed at all. The answer is that, although a single figure has very limited use, comparison of several values of the same ratio can be very helpful. Comparison can be carried out in two ways.

One is to compare the firm's results with that of another, or others. There are two difficulties, and the first of these, finding a truly comparable firm, has already been discussed. The second difficulty is that firms do not usually exchange information of this nature, especially with potential competitors. So we usually fall back on the second way.

Exhibit 18.2 gives figures for two years. It is valuable to compare the performance of Year Y with that of Y − 1. Next year we shall have three sets of figures Y − 1, Y, Y + 1. Generally we need four or five years' figures to make useful comparisons. We are using two years' figures for explanatory purposes only, not because it is a realistic thing to do.

Examination of Exhibit 18.2 ratio by ratio shows the following results:

Net Operating Return has increased. Notice that it has not increased by 1.2% but by 8%. The difference between the two figures is $16.2 - 15.0 = 1.2$. But this difference is the increase over 15%. As a percentage this works out at:

$$\frac{1.2}{15} \times 100 = 8\%.$$

There has been an 8% increase in the rate of profit. People look at two percentage figures, take one from the other, and call this "a percentage increase/decrease". It is not. This firm has had quite a good increase in profitability, which should not be hidden by use of an incorrect figure of 1.2%.

In spite of an 8% increase in NOR there has been a 4% fall in ROI.

$$\left(22.5 - 21.6 = 0.9; \quad \frac{0.9}{22.5} \times 100 = 4\% \right)$$

Profit has increased by £2, but the owner's investment has increased by £11. What is important to the owner is the amount earned for him. The falling rate of return suggests that the additional capital investment of £11 has not produced as high a return as the first £40. Perhaps this is to be expected; as a firm grows sales of the more profitable products cannot necessarily be increased continuously. As less profitable products are added to the line, overall profitability will fall. A subsidiary calculation will help.

The increase in profit is $(11 - 9) = £2$. In capital it is $(51 - 40) = £11$. Express these as a percentage:

$$\frac{\text{Increase in Profit}}{\text{Increase in Capital}} \times 100 = \frac{2}{11} \times 100 = 18.2\%$$

The increased capital is earning at a lower rate 18.2%. Presumably the rate for further additions of capital will fall even further. The owner must decide at what point to cease further investment.

In our example both short-term liquidity measures show improvement, WCR by 32% and LCR by 50%. Big improvements indeed. But whilst it is correct to prefer the highest rate obtainable for measures of profitability the same is not true of short-term liquidity.

Firms make profit out of the buying and selling of goods or the processing of raw materials into finished goods. A firm which raised its capital, paid it into a bank current account and left it at that would make no profit. Obviously firms would not behave like this deliberately but they may well find themselves in this position accidentally. The cash balance of our imaginary firm increased by 500% in one year. If this cash cannot be used to increase output and sales it should be put to some other use. All over the safe minimum could be used to repay borrowing. As this will reduce interest charges it will also increase ROI. So although the improved WCR and LCR indicate a greater cash safety margin care should be exercised if there is further "improvement" next year.

Finally the long-term liquidity measure shows a reduction in borrowing. One-third borrowed capital has decreased to one-quarter. Putting it the other way the owner used to provide two-thirds of the capital; he now provides three-quarters.

Having looked at each ratio individually let us try and sum up the results of these two years.

"Operating" return has increased satisfactorily. The fall in ROI, coupled with substantial increases in short-term liquidity, raises questions about the amount of capital employed. Borrowing forms a reduced proportion of capital employed, and could perhaps be reduced still further.

There is one other comparison to be made. The figures have been Actual for $Y - 1$, and we have assumed that Budgeted figures for Y correspond with the Actual. In the real world we would not expect 100% agreement. By applying the analysis of this chapter to Budgeted and Actual figures important results, and relationships, may be revealed.

So much we can gather from the financial results of the firm. But of course these results depend upon the manufacturing and selling success of the firm. It is this examination of operational performance which is carried out in the next chapter.

19. MEASURING OPERATIONAL PERFORMANCE

Measuring financial performance involved analysis of the Final Accounts. Measuring operational performance requires analysis of more detailed figures. Again we will assume that Budgeted and Actual figures for Y coincide. The complete results are shown in Exhibit 19.1, and each result has an identifying letter. There are three things to notice initially.

OPERATING PERFORMANCE RATIOS

(A) $ROS = \dfrac{NOR}{SALES} \times 100 = 9.2\%$

ALL REMAINING FIGURES ARE EXPRESSED "PER £1000 OF SALES"
IN ALL CASES THE DENOMINATOR IS 119

LETTER	NUMERATOR	£	COMMENTS
(B)	TOTAL ASSETS	571	
(C)	FIXED ASSETS	395	
(D)	NET CURRENT ASSETS	176	B = C + D 571 = 395 + 176
(E)	STOCKS	92	E + F + G − H = D
(F)	DEBTORS	109	
(G)	CASH	50	
(H)	CREDITORS	76	DIFFERENCE DUE TO ROUNDING
(J)	DIRECT COST	412	
(K)	RAW MATERIALS	252	J = K + L 412 = 252 + 160
(L)	LABOUR	160	
(M)	OVERHEADS	496	
(N)	TOTAL COST	908	N = J + M 908 = 412 + 496

EXHIBIT 19.1

First, whereas financial ratios used various definitions of capital for denominators, performance is now measured by reference to Sales. Throughout, £119 is the denominator.

Secondly, apart from A, all ratios are measured in terms of "per

£1,000 of Sales". The resultant figures seem to hold more meaning than the use of decimals or percentage.

Finally, some of these figures are the sum of others. Thus:

$$C \qquad + D \qquad\qquad = B$$

Fixed assets + Net Current assets = Total assets
per 1,000   per 1,000   per 1,000

$$395 \qquad + 176 \qquad\qquad = 571$$

Sometimes rounding each individual figure to the nearest £1 gives differences; but these are not significant.

$$E \qquad + F \qquad + G \qquad - H \qquad = D$$

Stocks   + Debtors + Cash   − Creditors = Net Current
per 1,000   per 1,000   per 1,000   per 1,000   Assets per
                                                     1,000

$$92 \qquad + 109 \qquad + 50 \qquad - 76 \qquad = 175$$

The real figure is 176. It is not sufficient to distort the analysis.

Turning to the analysis we can use it in the same two ways as with the financial analysis. Our figures can be compared with those of comparable firms. The difficulties here have already been discussed so we will move directly to comparisons with previous years.

Ratio A, **Return on Sales (ROS)**, is a measure of efficiency whereas NOR is a measure of profitability. ROS tells us what proportion of total sales revenue the managers succeeded in keeping within the firm. The whole analysis can be used to pinpoint any large variation. If ROS is lower than expected, check down the list. It may be that J, K and N are higher than anticipated. Investigation may show that there was a large increase in raw material prices at the beginning of the year. This will adversely affect K, Raw Material per £1,000 of Sales. In time this affects the Direct Cost figure J, and Total Costs, N.

In that example there was nothing to be done; our only achievement has been to find out why ROS fell. But many cases will be found where action can be taken; very often this will occur in the area of overhead expenditure. This can as easily get "out of hand" in a small firm as in a large.

By the time these ratios are prepared all the expenditure will have taken place; the water will have flowed under the bridge. But at least we can stop the flow for future years! Remember too that for our ratios we used budgeted figures. Here again we can use budgeting for control purposes. Armed with the Budgeted Ratios we can undertake half-yearly or, preferably, quarterly checks. This will enable us to take remedial action as quickly as possible.

20. CONCLUSION

Those of you with sufficient staying power to have reached this chapter will have examined all the aspects of financial and cost accounts of importance to small firms.

It is hoped that those who keep virtually no records will have come to believe that there is a definite advantage in maintaining some account of their business. At the risk of repetition, the ability to collect money from debtors quickly could, alone, pay for any time and trouble involved in keeping a Sales Ledger. And this is just one example of many ways in which the firm's cash flow can be improved through simple record keeping.

Firms keeping records are probably gaining some of these advantages already. However they would perhaps find some areas for improvement. When we turn to costing we usually find more reason for concern.

Some small manufacturing firms have little idea of the cost of individual product lines. This leads to part of the output at least being sold at less than cost. In particular there is great confusion over the nature, and treatment, of overheads. Those unfamiliar with the contribution approach would do well to grasp its implications, and use it as a basis for their own costing system.

As far as planning is concerned it is hoped that the idea that it is not worth it in a small firm and that it is too complicated, have both been discredited.

So far, in this conclusion, attention has been focused on firms which can be regarded as having a less than satisfactory accounting system. Of course very many small concerns are already operating successful systems, and profiting accordingly. Even for these businesses it is hoped that some additional insights will have been gained.

Whatever your reasons for reading this book, and whatever the current state of your accounting system, the author hopes it has given you a clearer insight into the functions of your firm. If so your work from now on may prove not only more profitable but also more enjoyable.

NOTES

NOTES

NOTES

NOTES

NOTES